Successful Corporate Fund Raising

WILEY NONPROFIT LAW, FINANCE, AND MANAGEMENT SERIES

The Art of Planned Giving: Understanding Donors and the Culture of Giving by Douglas E. White

Beyond Fund Raising: New Strategies for Nonprofit Investment and Innovation by Kay Grace

Budgeting for Not-for-Profit Organizations by David Maddox

Charity, Advocacy, and the Law by Bruce R. Hopkins

The Complete Guide to Fund Raising Management by Stanley Weinstein

The Complete Guide to Nonprofit Management by Smith, Bucklin & Associates

Critical Issues in Fund Raising edited by Dwight Burlingame

Developing Affordable Housing: A Practical Guide for Nonprofit Organizations, Second Edition by Bennett L. Hecht

Faith-Based Management: Leading Organizations That Are Based on More than Just Mission by Peter Brinckerhoff

Financial and Accounting Guide for Not-for-Profit Organizations, Sixth Edition by Malvern J. Gross, Jr., Richard F. Larkin, Roger S. Bruttomesso, John J. McNally, PricewaterhouseCoopers LLP

Financial Empowerment: More Money for More Mission by Peter Brinckerhoff

Financial Management for Nonprofit Organizations by Jo Ann Hankin, Alan Seidner, and John Zietlow

Financial Planning for Nonprofit Organizations by Jody Blazek

The Fund Raiser's Guide to the Internet by Michael Johnston

Fund-Raising: Evaluating and Managing the Fund Development Process, Second Edition by James M. Greenfield

Fund-Raising Fundamentals: A Guide to Annual Giving for Professionals and Volunteers by James M. Greenfield

Fund-Raising Regulation: A State-by-State Handbook of Registration Forms, Requirements, and Procedures by Seth Perlman and Betsy Hills Bush

Grantseeker's Toolkit: A Comprehensive Guide to Finding Funding by Cheryl S. New and James Quick

High Performance Nonprofit Organizations: Managing Upstream for Greater Impact by Christine Letts, William Ryan, and Allen Grossman

Intermediate Sanctions: Curbing Nonprofit Abuse by Bruce R. Hopkins and D. Benson Tesdahl

International Fund Raising for Nonprofits by Thomas Harris

International Guide to Nonprofit Law by Lester A. Salamon and Stefan Toepler & Associates

Joint Ventures Involving Tax-Exempt Organizations, Second Edition by Michael I. Sanders

The Law of Fund-Raising, Second Edition by Bruce R. Hopkins

The Law of Tax-Exempt Healthcare Organizations by Thomas K. Hyatt and Bruce R. Hopkins

The Law of Tax-Exempt Organizations, Seventh Edition by Bruce R. Hopkins

The Legal Answer Book for Nonprofit Organizations by Bruce R. Hopkins

A Legal Guide to Starting and Managing a Nonprofit Organization, Second Edition by Bruce R. Hopkins

Managing Affordable Housing: A Practical Guide to Creating Stable Communities by Bennett L. Hecht, Local Initiatives Support Corporation, and James Stockard

Managing Upstream: Creating High-Performance Nonprofit Organizations by Christine W. Letts, William P. Ryan, and Allan Grossman

Mission-Based Management: Leading Your Not-for-Profit Into the 21st Century by Peter Brinckerhoff

Mission-Based Marketing: How Your Not-for-Profit Can Succeed in a More Competitive World by Peter Brinckerhoff

Nonprofit Boards: Roles, Responsibilities, and Performance by Diane J. Duca

Nonprofit Compensation and Benefits Practices by Applied Research and Development Institute International, Inc.

Nonprofit Compensation, Benefits, and Employment Law by David G. Samuels and Howard Pianko

The Nonprofit Counsel by Bruce R. Hopkins

The Nonprofit Guide to the Internet, Second Edition by Michael Johnston

The Nonprofit Handbook, Second Edition:Volume I—Management by Tracy Daniel Connors

The Nonprofit Handbook, Second Edition:Volume II—Fund Raising by Jim Greenfield

Nonprofit Investment Policies: A Practical Guide to Creation and Implementation by Robert Fry, Jr.

The Nonprofit Law Dictionary by Bruce R. Hopkins

Nonprofit Litigation: A Practical Guide with Forms and Checklists by Steve Bachmann

The Nonprofit Manager's Resource Dictionary by Ronald A. Landskroner

Nonprofit Organizations' Business Forms: Disk Edition by John Wiley & Sons, Inc.

Planned Giving: Management, Marketing, and Law, Second Edition by Ronald R. Jordan and Katelyn L. Quynn

Private Foundations: Tax Law and Compliance by Bruce R. Hopkins and Jody Blazek

Program Related Investments: A Technical Manual for Foundations by Christie I. Baxter

Reengineering Your Nonprofit Organization: A Guide to Strategic Transformation by Alceste T. Pappas

Reinventing the University: Managing and Financing Institutions of Higher Education by Sandra L. Johnson and Sean C. Rush, PricewaterhouseCoopers LLP

The Second Legal Answer Book for Nonprofit Organizations by Bruce R. Hopkins

Special Events: Proven Strategies for Nonprofit Fund Raising by Alan Wendroff

Strategic Communications for Nonprofit Organizations: Seven Steps to Creating a Successful Plan by Janel Radtke

Strategic Planning for Nonprofit Organizations: A Practical Guide and Workbook by Michael Allison and Jude Kaye, Support Center for Nonprofit Management

Streetsmart Financial Basics for Nonprofit Managers by Thomas A. McLaughlin

A Streetsmart Guide to Nonprofit Mergers and Networks by Thomas A. McLaughlin

Successful Marketing Strategies for Nonprofit Organizations by Barry J. McLeish

The Tax Law of Charitable Giving, Second Edition by Bruce R. Hopkins

The Tax Law of Colleges and Universities by Bertrand M. Harding

Tax Planning and Compliance for Tax-Exempt Organizations: Forms, Checklists, Procedures, Third Edition by Jody Blazek

The Universal Benefits of Volunteering: A Practical Workbook for Nonprofit Organizations, Volunteers and Corporations by Walter P. Pidgeon, Jr.

The Volunteer Management Handbook by Tracy Daniel Connors

Successful Corporate Fund Raising

Effective Strategies for Today's Nonprofits

K. Scott Sheldon

JOHN WILEY & SONS, INC.

New York • Chichester • Weinheim • Brisbane • Singapore • Toronto

Library of Congress Cataloging-in-Publication Data:

Sheldon, K. Scott.
    Successful corporate fund raising : effective strategies for today's nonprofits / K. Scott Sheldon.
        p.   cm.
    Includes bibliographical references and index.
    ISBN 0-471-35016-8 (cloth)
    1. Fund raising—United States. 2. Corporations—Charitable contributions— United States. I. Title.

HV41.9.U5 S535 2000
658.15'224—dc21

                                                                                    99-049065

The author wishes to dedicate this book to the growing number of credit and non-credit certificate and degree programs in nonprofit management that are taking hold at colleges and universities across the United States and in other countries. In particular, I wish to dedicate this book to the faculty and developers of one such program, the Certificate in Fund Raising Management Program, launched in the mid-1970s by Adelphi University on Long Island. Where I am today in my professional career is due in no small part to the education and guidance conveyed by this pioneering group of inspired individuals. To all of you, I say thank you.

About the Author

K. Scott Sheldon has been engaged in fund raising for educational institutions, both at the independent school and university level, since 1977. He has written numerous articles and given lectures on various aspects of corporate fund raising including featured presentations at the National Society of Fund Raising Executives' (NSFRE) International Conference on Fund Raising. A Certified Fund Raising Executive, Mr. Sheldon was honored as the Outstanding Fund Raising Executive of the year by the California Capital Chapter of NSFRE in 1991. After graduating from Adelphi University's Fund Raising Management Certificate Program in 1976, he began his career in New York City as Assistant Director of Development of the Dalton School. He holds a BS in Economics from the Wharton School of the University of Pennsylvania and an MBA in Marketing from New York University's Stern School of Business. Mr. Sheldon currently serves on the board of directors of the Greater Arizona Chapter of NSFRE. At present, he is Director of Development and Outreach for the College of Extended Education at Arizona State University in Tempe, Arizona. In this capacity, he has responsibility for all aspects of the College's fund raising, including securing support for ASU's Nonprofit Management Institute.

Preface

Successful Corporate Fund Raising: Effective Strategies for Today's Nonprofits is designed with one overriding purpose in mind: to help nonprofit organizations create effective corporate fund-raising programs. The book is written with an eye toward the large number of nonprofits that have limited time, staff, and resources to devote to corporate philanthropy, let alone all other types of fund raising. By some estimates there are close to one million nonprofit organizations in the United States, more than triple the number that existed in 1970. Many of these agencies have annual budgets well below $1 million. And yet these organizations, perhaps more so than some large, national nonprofits, need help in developing effective, low-cost strategies to solicit much-needed corporate support.

It is important for nonprofit agencies to note that corporate support of the nonprofit sector amounts to less than 10 percent of all funds contributed each year in the United States. The majority of the philanthropic dollar comes from, and will continue to come from, individuals. Nonetheless, corporate support can be significant to some organizations, particularly in the form of non-cash and in-kind contributions.

It is not the intention of this book to focus on the theoretical aspects of corporate giving nor to engage in a conversation on the merits of corporate philanthropy. Rather, the book emphasizes a practical, hands-on approach to securing corporate support. It is the author's sincere hope that the reader, at a minimum, will learn several new techniques and ideas that can then be incorporated into the overall corporate solicitation strategy for his or her agency.

Alternatively, someone new to corporate fund raising may find this book an invaluable guide in helping to launch and maintain a successful corporate development program.

Acknowledgments

The author wishes to acknowledge the founders of the National Society of Fund Raising Executives for having the vision to create an organization dedicated to bringing professionalism and ethics to the fund-raising profession. The author also wishes to thank the following individuals who either served as mentors and/or nurtured the creativity and imagination that the author has brought to the fund-raising process: Rod Pellett, Bob Semple, Dennis Hartzell, Ernie Wood, and Bette DeGraw. Finally, the author wishes to thank in particular his editor at John Wiley & Sons, Martha Cooley, for her gentle ongoing persistence without which, quite honestly, this book would probably still be unfinished.

Contents

Introduction

Successful Corporate Fund Raising: Effective Strategies for Today's Nonprof-its begins with an overall look at corporate giving in the United States, followed by a review and understanding of corporate America's inter-est in supporting the nonprofit community and the corporate sector's embrace of strategic philanthropy, and then a discussion of the three major types of support that companies provide to nonprofits: cash sup-port, non-cash support, and volunteerism.

Following a description of how companies provide support, we will look at the corporate fund-raising process, beginning with research, moving through cultivation and solicitation, and ending with evalua-tion and stewardship.

Each section of the book provides in-depth information on a certain aspect of corporate giving and then follows up with strategies that nonprofits can employ to successfully attract corporate support.

We will also look at who the decision makers are within the corporate hierarchy and how technology is having a profound impact on the sec-tor. Again, in each case, we will examine simple, cost-effective strategies that nonprofits can pursue to increase their share of today's consider-able corporate support dollar.

Near the conclusion of the book, a case study is provided which high-lights employee matching gifts and how to maximize success in this area.

Ultimately, the reader should be able to take the information gleaned from this book and use it to create and implement a realistic, sound strategy to raise corporate dollars within an agency's overall fund-raising program.

The Background

Chapter One   Introduction to Corporate Giving

Chapter Two   The Philosophy of Corporate Giving

OVERVIEW

This book is designed to give the reader a hands-on, practical guide to attracting corporate support to a nonprofit agency. First, however, it is important to have an understanding of corporate giving in general and how it fits into the overall world of organized philanthropy.

In Section One we will explore the history of corporate giving and look at a number of statistical indicators that compare corporate giving to giving by individuals, estates, and foundations. We will determine that while corporate giving is quite significant, it still represents only a small slice of the total philanthropic dollar.

After reviewing the current status of the size and magnitude of corporate giving, we will spend some time gaining a better understanding and appreciation of the philosophy of corporate giving. That is, why do corporations give at all? What motivates them to support the nonprofit sector?

Finally, we will learn the importance of nonprofit agencies seeking corporate support, and their adapting to current corporate philosophy and corporate giving to succeed in today's competitive grants marketplace.

CHAPTER ONE

Introduction to Corporate Giving

Organized corporate support of the nonprofit sector in America has grown rapidly in the past several decades. According to Giving USA, an annual compendium of statistical information on the state of philanthropy in the United States, total corporate giving in 1997 totaled $8.2 billion. This figure includes support identified as charitable in nature, meaning the company sought, in most instances, a charitable tax deduction for its generosity. It does not include so-called strategic support of nonprofits, which can include funding from corporate budgets such as marketing, advertising, research, and promotion which many times is not earmarked as a charitable contribution by the company.

Corporate giving has, and continues, to grow. Giving USA, published by the AAFRC Trust for Philanthropy, reports that total corporate giving has increased ten-fold in the last thirty years. And yet, while the $8 billion that companies contributed annually to the nonprofit sector in the late 1990s may sound significant (and it certainly is!) it represents only 5.7 percent (including giving by both companies and company-sponsored foundations) of all the money contributed in the United States each year. By far the largest single provider of the charitable dollar has come from, and continues to come from, individuals.

Let's look at who provides charitable support in America today as noted in Exhibit 1.1.

Exhibit 1.1   Sources of Charitable Support in America

Group	Dollars	Percentage
Individuals	$ 109.3 billion	76.2%
Bequests	$ 12.6 billion	8.8%
Foundations	$ 13.4 billion	9.3%
Corporations	$ 8.2 billion	5.7%
Total	$ 143.5 billion	100%

Source: Giving USA, 1998.

While total corporate giving in the United States represents the smallest portion of the philanthropic pie, when compared to individuals and foundations, corporate support of the nonprofit sector has been experiencing accelerating growth in the late 1990s. This compares favorably to the late 1980s and early 1990s when corporate giving was essentially flat on a year over year basis.

Exhibit 1.2 shows both the total dollars contributed each year from 1992 to 1997 by corporations to charity and the annual percentage change each year.

Note that the average annual percentage increase from 1995 to 1997 is approximately 6.3 percent compared to the approximately 5.9 percent average annual increase for the prior three year period. Therefore, the average annual percentage increase was about 7 percent higher in 1995 to 1997 as compared to 1992 to 1994.

Corporations provide support to a variety of nonprofit organizations. In a trend that mirrors giving by individuals, the largest beneficiary of corporate support, as noted in Exhibit 1.3, is education, followed fairly closely by health and human service agencies.

Exhibit 1.2   Annual Growth in Corporate Philanthropy 1992–1997

Year	Amount Contributed	Percentage Increase Over Previous Year
1992	$ 5.91 billion	2.0%
1993	$ 6.26 billion	5.9%
1994	$ 6.88 billion	9.9%
1995	$ 7.40 billion	7.6%
1996	$ 8.00 billion	8.1%
1997	$ 8.25 billion	3.1%

Source: Giving USA, 1998.

Exhibit 1.3   Who Receives Corporate Donations?

Category	Percentage
Arts/Culture	9%
Education	30%
Health/Human Services	25%
Civic/Community	10%
Other	9%
Unallocated	17%
Total	100%

Source: Giving USA, 1998.

THE CORPORATE GIVING STRUCTURE

Companies employ several structures through which they direct their corporate philanthropy. For most companies this is accomplished by either direct corporate giving or through a separate, more formalized structure, known as a corporate foundation, sometimes referred to as a company-sponsored foundation.

Some companies only make grants through direct giving programs, while others only support nonprofits via a corporate foundation. In some instances, a company may have both a direct corporate giving program and a corporate foundation through which to direct its charitable support. As we will see, direct corporate giving is the most popular structure used by corporate America today.

Exhibit 1.4 helps to conceptualize the three giving structures.

Many companies in the United States, both small and large, have no corporate giving structure in place. If they give at all to the nonprofit sector it is through a very informal process done usually at the discretion of the company CEO, founder, or owner.

Exhibit 1.4   Corporate Giving Organizational Structures

Direct Corporate Giving	Giving via Company Sponsored Foundation	Hybrid Giving Structure	
The Company Provides Only Direct Support	The Company Provides Support Only Through Its Foundation	The Company Provides Both	
		Direct Support	and Foundation Support
$	$	$	$
$	$	$	$
$	$	$	$
$	$	$	$
Nonprofit	Nonprofit	Nonprofit	Nonprofit

DIRECT CORPORATE GIVING

In the direct corporate giving structure, companies identify nonprofit agencies they wish to support and direct gifts to these agencies. Direct cash giving by corporations is far and away the single largest method through which companies support the nonprofit sector and accounts for about 75 percent of overall total corporate giving in the United States today.

Direct corporate giving is a process through which companies with an expressed desire in helping the nonprofit sector channel their corporate cash support. Some companies have very structured, rigid corporate giving policies and guidelines while others may provide funding with the simple verbal approval of the company's CEO or president. In later sections we will explore the ways to approach corporations for a gift and learn who the primary decision makers are within the corporate contributions hierarchy.

CORPORATE FOUNDATIONS

A more formalized approach toward corporate giving occurs when a company establishes what is commonly referred to as a corporate foundation. A corporate foundation is subject to more stringent reporting regulations since the foundation is subject to scrutiny by the Internal Revenue Service.

Some History

Some corporate foundations were launched more than a half-century ago. One example is the UPS Foundation, which will celebrate its fiftieth anniversary in 2001, and which was created by the United Parcel Service Company. The UPS Foundation is the structure that UPS has chosen to provide financial support to the nonprofit sector. The first corporate foundation ever to be established in the United States is generally credited to be the Dayton Corporation, now known as the Dayton Hudson Corporation. The Dayton Corporation established the Dayton Foundation in 1918. Other companies that set up foundations prior to 1935 were Sears Roebuck, Bausch & Lomb, and Lincoln National Life Insurance Company. What is perhaps interesting to point out as a historical footnote is that these foundations, when they were launched, were making gifts that provided no tax advantage to the company. It was not until 1936 that the forerunner of today's Internal Revenue

Service allowed companies to claim a charitable deduction for their philanthropic support of the nonprofit sector.

A corporate foundation derives its funds from its corporate parent but is set up to be independent of the parent company. The Foundation Center, a New York-based organization that specializes in collecting and disseminating information on U.S. foundations, reported that in 1996 there were 41,500 grant making foundations in the United States of which 1,970, or 4.7 percent, were set up as corporate foundations. In total, these corporate foundations provided just under $2 billion in grants in 1996. Recall that total corporate giving in the United States in the late 1990s was roughly $8 billion per year. Thus, we can see that three-quarters, or 75 percent, of all corporate giving is direct in nature: that is, it is made outside of a company-sponsored foundation.

Exhibit 1.5 shows the total dollar breakdown between direct corporate giving and giving via a corporate foundation for 1996.

Company foundations only make outright cash grants (or pledges paid over time) to nonprofit agencies, usually limited to what are called 501(c)(3) organizations as defined by the Internal Revenue Service. The size of corporate foundations vary widely both in terms of their assets and the amount of grants that are distributed on an annual basis. See Exhibit 1.6. At one extreme there are a handful of very large corporate foundations while at the other end are a sizeable number of small foundations.

Company-sponsored foundations are subject to the same rules that apply to private foundations, among which is the requirement that the company foundation distribute funds totaling at least 5 percent of assets each year. Company foundations, for the most part, are quite dependent on the economy since, typically, the amount that the foundation receives annually from the parent company will depend on the company's earnings from the prior year. Thus, there can be wide swings from one year to the next on how much a corporate foundation may be able to provide in the way of contributions. This uncertainty can make planning difficult for both the funder and the nonprofit organizations that depend on the funder's support.

Exhibit 1.5 Comparing Direct Corporate Giving to Corporate Foundations

Type	Amount	Percentage
Direct Corporate Giving	$ 6.2 billion	77.5%
Giving via Corporate Foundation	$ 1.8 billion	22.5%
Total	$ 8.0 billion	100.0%

Source: The Foundation Center and Giving USA, 1997.

Exhibit 1.6   Corporate Foundations Based on Total Grants Paid

Total Grants Paid Annually	Number of Foundations	Percentage of All Corporate Foundations
Under $100,000	923	46.8%
$100,000–$1,000,000	699	35.5%
Over $1,000,000	347	17.7%
Total	1,969	100%

Source: The Foundation Center, 1997.

Not all company foundations, however, are subject to the vagaries of the economy. Some forward thinking companies (Minneapolis-based General Mills, for example) have separated the funding of their corporate foundations from yearly swings in corporate profits. These companies fund their corporate foundations at the same level each year thus making for smoother and more predictable charitable gift planning.

Reatha Clark King, the executive director for the General Mills Foundation, predicted at a 1998 meeting of the Arizona Grant Makers Association and the Arizona-based Valley Contributors Network that the rate of formation of newly established corporate foundations in America will actually decrease in the years ahead. For those companies with foundations, King believes that we are likely to see a conversion of such foundations into direct corporate giving programs. King's reasoning is simple: direct corporate giving is much more flexible and can adapt more readily to changing economic conditions. It is also subject to much less government scrutiny than corporate foundations.

OTHER TYPES OF CORPORATE SUPPORT

It has become popular in recent years for corporate America to augment its traditional philanthropic support of the nonprofit sector with additional funding from other budgets within the company. These include dollars set aside from budget lines established for marketing, public relations, promotion, and research. We will look at these types of corporate support in more detail in Chapter 3.

CONCLUSION

Contrary to current public opinion there is much good news to report on the growth of corporate giving in America today. While corporate support of the nonprofit sector slowed considerably during the recession of the early 1990s, it witnessed accelerated annualized growth in the second half of the decade. If the past is any predictor of the future, it should be safe to say that corporate philanthropy will continue to be a significant source of support for America's nonprofit community for many years to come.

In Chapter 2 we will review the philosophy of corporate giving from the corporate point of view and how it has changed over time. Then, in Section Two, we will review the three major types of support that most nonprofit organizations can successfully obtain from the corporate community: cash support, non-cash support, and corporate volunteers. In later chapters we will look at how best to approach a company for support and explore in detail the various decision makers within a company and how they decide on the distribution of funds to nonprofit agencies.

CHAPTER TWO

The Philosophy of Corporate Giving

OVERVIEW

In this chapter we will review the philosophy of corporate giving from the viewpoint of the funder: the corporation. Nonprofits that are able to adapt most easily to the current philosophy of corporate giving will find that they are in a position to succeed in garnering their fair share of the corporate philanthropic pie.

CORPORATE AMERICA

Corporate America's attitude toward support of the nonprofit sector has changed over the years. In the past, a company's philanthropic program was often a reflection of the charitable attitude of the company president or chief executive officer. In addition, corporate support was most often directed at traditional nonprofit agencies in the community that provided important social services. Many times the same charities would receive funding each year simply because they had received similar support in years past. Giving was purely philanthropic and not tied to company business objectives.

GOOD CORPORATE CITIZEN

These days, the words good corporate citizen are often used by corporate executives to explain why they feel it is important for their respective companies to give back to the community. As a very recent example, in 1999, BMW of North America, a division of the large German automaker, adopted the Susan G. Komen Breast Cancer Foundation as one of the company's main charities of choice. In a prepared statement the President of BMW of North America said that breast cancer was a serious health concern that affected hundreds of thousands of women in the United States and that this was one very visible way that the company could give back to the community.

In addition to being viewed as good corporate citizens, most company executives feel that any corporate support should go to nonprofits in areas in which the company has operations and/or where the company's employees live or work.

This attitude is reflected in the recent remarks of Douglas Leatherdale, chairman, president, and CEO of the St. Paul Companies, when he said "We are committed to community involvement in the communities where we live and do business."

PROACTIVE CORPORATE PHILANTHROPY

As part of the overall evolution of corporate giving there has been a very definite shift away from traditional reactive philanthropy to a much more proactive, strategic approach. In the reactive model, company executives basically responded with gifts of cash only after being solicited by a nonprofit. In the proactive model, company officials often pre-identify organizations with which they wish to be associated and work with these agencies to provide a mix of support options that could include, for example, a loaned executive, sponsorship dollars from the public relations budget, and a below market-rate loan for capital improvements.

An Example of the Proactive Corporate Giving Model

The national brokerage firm Merrill Lynch is an example of a company pursuing a very aggressive proactive approach to corporate giving. The company encourages its district managers to pick a local or regional nonprofit agency that they want to be affiliated with in the community. Then, the company's public relations department contacts the selected nonprofit agency to identify ways in which the company can be an active participant.

This participation may include sponsorship dollars and having the district manager join the agency's board. It could also include a localized cause-related marketing initiative.

Seeds for Proactive Giving Date Back to the 1970s

The movement toward more focused corporate strategic philanthropy, while accelerating, is certainly not new. The seeds for a more proactive approach to corporate philanthropy emerged in the 1970s when corporate America first realized it was part of a global economy in which U.S. companies would be competing on a much larger playing field.

In 1981, Don Moody, then executive director of the Fort Worth Clearing House in Texas, stated at a meeting of the Ft. Worth chapter of the National Society of Fund Raising Executives that "corporations are looking for cost/benefit gift relationships." These comments were an early sign indicative of a shift toward strategic philanthropy. In the 1960s you would not have heard such a statement because at that time, giving was often based on the personal preferences of the company president without any thought of whether such a gift was strategic or complemented the company's business plan.

Exhibit 2.1 lists some questions that corporations are likely to ask in today's competitive grant environment when determining what nonprofits the company is likely to support.

Cone Communications, a well known Boston-based consulting firm that specializes in strategic philanthropy says "companies can and should do well while doing good. Companies who understand that the strategic interaction of social issues is an essential business practice will come to define the most successful companies and brands in the twenty-first century."

Exhibit 2.1 Sample Questions Asked by Corporate Funders

Will the giving generate publicity?

Will it associate us with a good cause?

Are there sufficient opportunities for employee involvement?

Will it create a base of future customers?

Source: "Nonprofits Must Have Smart Marketing Plans," *The Puget Sound Business Journal*, April 13, 1998.

Strategic philanthropy has taken quite a hold in corporate America today. Many companies now embrace the philosophy of defining effective corporate philanthropy as the process of melding the company's business objectives with a community's social issues to the extent that this can be achieved.

COMPANY'S CORPORATE VALUE SYSTEM IMPACTS CHARITABLE GIVING

There is no doubt that a company's approach to and interest in philanthropy depends in large part on whether it is considered a core value of the company and its employees. All companies fall on a continuum when it comes to philanthropy, ranging from absolutely no interest in (and perhaps even resistance to) giving to a commitment to helping nonprofits as much as possible, and whether this attitude is prevalent at all ranks within the organization, ranging from the executive suite all the way down to the receiving dock. Some companies, notably the Charles Schwab Company, to name just one (although there are many others), inculcate a spirit of philanthropy in almost all facets of the company's business operations.

NONPROFIT'S ATTITUDE TOWARDS CORPORATE GIVING

In general, most nonprofits believe that soliciting support from the nonprofit community should be part of their overall fund-raising strategy. However, in reality, many nonprofits, particularly smaller ones, either don't devote any resources to corporate fund-raising initiatives or only provide minimal support.

There are several reasons for this. In smaller nonprofits there is usually only one person, more often than not working at less than full-time status, who has responsibilities for all of the agency's fund-raising activities. This person's time is directed mostly at cultivating and soliciting individuals who are close to the organization, leaving little time for corporate solicitation.

Also, many nonprofit organizations are uncomfortable with corporate fund raising in large part because they do not understand the process. Without an understanding of who and how to approach a company, little progress is made. Also, some agencies have tried sporadically to raise funds from companies with little success. Thus, they tend to believe that corporate fund raising provides little return on investment and direct their time and resources to areas that are perceived to provide a higher return. Alternatively, the agency mistakenly believes that corporate America will not support their nonprofit's cause because it is not mainstream or is perceived as being controversial.

For any kind of nonprofit there are those that will be successful with corporate giving and those that will not. The secret to success, regardless of the agency type or cause, is to design and engage in an effective, sustainable corporate fund-raising program that seeks to work with today's corporate philanthropy objectives.

WORKING TOGETHER

Both nonprofits and the corporate community need to work together to make the most of corporate America's interest in supporting the nonprofit sector. Those nonprofits that embrace the concept of strategic philanthropy and develop strategies to tap into this business model will succeed in the years to come.

CONCLUSION

In this chapter we have reviewed the current attitude that companies have adopted with regard to their philanthropy. Most, though not all, people agree that corporate support of the nonprofit sector is appropriate. Nonprofits need to work closely with companies to find ways to obtain corporate support and, at the same time, help companies to be viewed as good corporate citizens.

In Section Two we will explore the three primary ways that companies provide support to the nonprofit community: cash support, noncash support, and volunteers.

SECTION TWO

Types of Support

Chapter Three   Direct Cash Support

Chapter Four   In-Kind Support

Chapter Five   Corporate Volunteerism

OVERVIEW

How Companies Support the Nonprofit Sector

In the first section of this book we reviewed the significant amount of support that corporate America provides to the nonprofit sector. We also explored in detail the philosophy on which current corporate giving is based. In this section we will review the types of support companies provide.

If you pick up a recent corporate annual report that includes a section on corporate citizenship, as many annual reports do these days, you will see that companies tend to group their donations into three distinct areas: cash contributions, in-kind (or non-cash) donations, and employee volunteerism. All three types of giving will be explored in depth in this section.

Traditional Giving Model

Corporate philanthropy continues to evolve over time. This overview will explain the difference between the traditional corporate model and the new corporate model. Some years ago the only type of support provided by most companies was in the form of traditional cash gifts. The early seeds of corporate giving were planted in 1936 when the Internal Revenue Service, for the first time, allowed companies to take a charitable tax deduction, or write-off, for supporting certain types of nonprofit organizations.

The New Corporate Giving Model

Corporate giving today is much more varied and diverse than at any time in our history. Today, companies may make both traditional cash contributions from a philanthropic budget and augment this with support from other corporate budgets not specifically earmarked for charitable purposes. In addition, this cash support can be supplemented with in-kind support and the use of employee volunteers. A comparison of the traditional versus the new model follows:

Traditional Model	New Model
• Cash gifts	• Cash support and/or
	• In-kind support and/or
	• Employee volunteers

In the next three chapters we will look at each of the three areas of the new corporate giving model, beginning with a discussion of cash support of the nonprofit sector.

CHAPTER THREE

Direct Cash Support

Corporations contribute several billions of dollars in direct cash gifts to nonprofit organizations each year, representing the bulk of the support that companies provide to the nonprofit sector.

Each year, the Michigan-based Taft Group identifies the top ten corporate cash donors. Exhibit 3.1 shows the top ten corporate donors for 1997.

The top ten corporate givers, combined, contribute close to a half-billion dollars each year or about six percent of the total given by all U.S. companies. The list is heavily weighted on companies that were created during America's industrial revolution. However, note the presence of several new companies that represent the future direction of the United States in both communications and information: Intel and AT&T. Obviously, the list of top ten companies will change each year. In all likelihood we will see a shift in the make-up of the top ten with more representation from so-called Information age companies as the twenty-first century progresses.

WHO RECEIVES SUPPORT?

Typically, nonprofits selected for corporate support are located in areas in which the company has operations and/or in which the company's employees live and work. While still independent, the telecommunications giant, Sprint Corp., now part of WorldCom, preferred to contribute

Exhibit 3.1　The Top Ten Cash Givers for 1997

Company	Total Cash Giving
General Motors	$ 58.9 million
Exxon Corp.	$ 55.4 million
Ford Motor Company	$ 52.0 million
General Electric Co.	$ 50.1 million
Johnson & Johnson	$ 49.4 million
AT&T Corporation	$ 48.3 million
Intel Corporation	$ 46.7 million
Procter & Gamble Co.	$ 46.6 million
Dayton-Hudson	$ 45.8 million
Boeing Co.	$ 42.5 million

Source: The Taft Group's Corporate Giving Directory, 20th Edition, 1997.

to agencies where the company had operations as exemplified in this passage from the company's contributions guidelines: "The Sprint Foundation's charitable giving program emphasizes support of local and regional organizations in those communities in which the company has a major presence. Subsidiaries and regional offices administer their own charitable giving programs. Contact the public relations department of the nearest office for more information."

Some companies will support any type of legitimate nonprofit organization while others prefer to limit their support to a particular type of nonprofit such as those involved in education, the arts, or health and human services.

SOURCES OF CORPORATE FUNDING

The funds that corporations allocate for nonprofit support can come from a number of sources within the company. Some are created for the specific and sole purpose of making charitable, tax-deductible contributions to nonprofit agencies. Others, like the marketing budget, might be tapped occasionally to provide support to a nonprofit that the company has chosen to align itself with. Exhibit 3.2 compares the traditional philanthropic budgets within a company to other budget areas a company might wish to utilize. In today's economy companies are much more likely to tap into non-traditional non-philanthropic budgets to enhance their support of the nonprofit sector.

We will now take a look at each type of cash support that a company typically makes to a nonprofit organization.

Exhibit 3.2   Corporate Budgets That Support the Nonprofit Sector

Traditional Philanthropic Budgets Provide	Other Corporate Budgets* Accessed to Support Nonprofits
Direct Corporate Grants**	Marketing
	Public Relations
	Research & Development
	Sr. Management Discretionary Funds
Company Sponsored Foundation Grants**	Advertising
	Sales

*Company may or may not consider this type of support to be a charitable contribution.

**Includes support for employee matching gift programs, to be discussed later.

GRANTS

The first and most traditional type of corporate philanthropic support comes in the form of grants that an agency applies for through a competitive application process. This is the method that a nonprofit would use when approaching a corporate foundation, a special grant making entity created by the company. The same holds true when approaching a company that makes grants via direct corporate giving. In a later section we will talk in some detail about the proposal process and what the company requires from an applicant.

Of all the types of cash support provided by a company, the largest single type is made via a competitive grants process. This is the most formalized type of support and comes from budgets specifically set up for this purpose. Not all companies have structured philanthropic programs. In fact, quite the opposite is true. There are many more companies in America that have no structured charitable program than those that do. One purpose of this book is to help you identify those companies that do so that you can spend your time and resources as productively as possible.

EMPLOYEE MATCHING GIFT PROGRAMS

As part of the funds that companies set aside for traditional, philanthropic support of the nonprofit sector, a number of companies have established employee matching gift programs. The company agrees to match gifts made by their employees. The most common match is on a one-for-one ratio. Thus, if an employee makes a personal gift of $100 to an arts organization and then completes the appropriate paperwork, his or her employer will also make a contribution of $100 to the same arts organization. The match ratio varies by company. Some companies will match on a two-for-one or even three-for-one basis.

At present, over 6,000 companies in the United States, both public and private, have employee matching gift programs. Several organizations sell reference guides listing detailed information of these programs. These organizations are discussed in Chapter 13. In some ways, matching gifts are like found money. As long as the employee makes a gift, the employer will single, double, or triple-match the contribution, thus giving the agency a significant return on the original gift without too much additional effort.

GE Established First Matching Gift Program

The first corporate matching gift program to be established in the United States can be credited to the General Electric Company, which launched its matching gift program in the early 1950s. For more than 40 years, GE has faithfully matched literally thousands of gifts made by its employees. Today, GE is currently at the forefront of using technology to streamline the matching gift process. The company now allows employees to avoid filling out time consuming paperwork and, in its place, initiate the matching gift process simply by using a touch tone phone. A list of companies using phone automated systems for employee matching gifts appears in Appendix C.

Many companies have followed in GE's footprints over the years. Even Japanese companies with operations in the United States now encourage employees to make matching gifts. The Mitsubishi Electric America Foundation provides both outright matching grants that supplement cash, products, and employee volunteer time donated by the company's employees and additional matching gifts that match individual employee donations to qualified charitable organizations.

Matching Gift Programs Viewed as Democratic

Employee matching gift programs are viewed by the corporate sector as a uniquely democratic way to support nonprofit organizations since the decision on who to support is first made by the employee. Also, because of the importance of such programs, most companies are very hesitant to curtail employee matching gifts even in an economic downturn. Thus, matching gift programs have a protected status in recessions, and while they may be modified (such as reducing the match ratio) they are rarely completely rescinded.

Naturally, there are some restrictions on corporate employee matching gift programs. Most companies will not make matching gifts to all types of nonprofits. The majority of companies tend to support educational institutions, including colleges and, to a lesser extent, community colleges and K-12 schools.

Companies Expand List of Qualifying Nonprofits

A number of nonprofits do not actively engage in seeking matching gifts because of the mistaken assumption that they will not qualify for a matching gift since they are not an educationally-oriented nonprofit. Over the past decade many companies have expanded the types of nonprofits that they will support via matching gift programs. Today, for example, it is not uncommon for a company to include arts and cultural organizations and health and human service organizations as eligible matching gift institutions. In fact, according to the 1998 edition of Giving USA, 15 percent of all companies with matching gift programs will match gifts made to any qualifying 501(c)(3) nonprofit organization.

Minimum Employee Gift Often Required

Some other restrictions on matching gift programs that nonprofits need to be aware of include minimum and maximum matching amounts. For example, many companies have set a minimum gift, typically $25, that an employee needs to make to have a gift matched. Conversely, there is often a maximum amount, such as $5,000 per employee per year.

We will take an in-depth look at matching gifts and how to employ a successful strategy to increase matching gift income in Chapter 13.

CAUSE-RELATED MARKETING

Many companies set aside a portion of their annual marketing budget to support nonprofit agencies. Marketing dollars are much more discretionary and flexible and follow a much less rigid review and decision-making process than those funds distributed through a company's traditional philanthropic grants program. One of the more common ways that companies allocate marketing dollars to the nonprofit sector is through arrangements that have come to be known as cause-related marketing relationships or agreements.

Cause-related marketing is a relatively recent development in philanthropic history. Essentially, cause-related marketing (CRM) tries to more closely align a company's philanthropy to usage by the public of the company's product line. According to Giving USA, "Cause-related marketing, though it is more marketing than a contributions strategy, does provide benefits to some nonprofits."

This notion is further reinforced by the findings of a Cone/Roper poll (as reported in *Giving USA*, 1996) taken in 1993 that "found that 71 percent of consumers believe cause-related marketing is a good way to solve social problems. Furthermore, 84 percent have a more positive image of a company if it is doing something to make the world a better place."

History of Cause-Related Marketing

The origin of cause-related marketing is often attributed to the American Express Company and its involvement in the renovation and refurbishment of the Statue of Liberty in the early 1980s. At that time, American Express announced that the company would provide a contribution to the renovation efforts each and every time an American Express cardholder used his or her card to make a purchase.

The American Express Travel Related Services Company, a division of the American Express Company, arranged to contribute the following amounts to the Statue of Liberty-Ellis Island restoration campaign: a penny each time one of the company's credit cards was used, $1 for every new card application that was approved, and $1 for every purchased vacation package that had a value of $500 or more. As a result of this campaign, card usage increased close to 30 percent, new card applications shot up and, ultimately, the company contributed $1.7 million to the project.

At the time, it proved to be a novel concept in philanthropy and went on to spur a number of such initiatives, with other companies and nonprofits linking together in similar programs. The concept works well with companies that are able to develop a marketing program with a charity that is national in scope.

Examples of Recent Cause-Related Marketing Initiatives

The list of companies that engage in cause-related marketing at some point in their life cycle continues to grow. In 1999, two companies (among many others) that agreed to support awareness of breast cancer were BMW of North America and the Charles Schwab Company. BMW agreed to provide $1 for every mile a BMW car was test-driven by a customer. Schwab donated the total on-line commission, $29.95, for every stock trade placed on Sunday, May 9, 1999. In both cases, the funds provided went to the Susan G. Komen Breast Cancer Foundation.

Locally-Based Cause-Related Marketing Is a Viable Option

Cause-related marketing is a viable option for many smaller nonprofits that do not have a national presence. Many local companies are willing to participate in a cause-related marketing initiative. For example, a local or regional hotel chain may be willing to partner with one or more local nonprofits in such a program. In this arrangement the hotel may promote its involvement with the charity through the hotel's own advertising and public relations department. The advertising would indicate that the hotel chain agreed to contribute a fixed amount to the featured nonprofit each time a person mentions that charity's name at check-in. Several years ago the Texas-based hotel chain, LaQuinta, established a cause-related marketing initiative with the American Cancer Society. LaQuinta agreed to contribute a certain dollar amount each time a patron chose to stay in a non-smoking room.

Another example of cause-related marketing on the local level is a tie-in with the Boise, Idaho-based grocery chain, Albertson's. This company encourages nonprofit agencies to distribute so-called "affinity" cards to clients and friends of the organization. Then, each time these individuals shop at Albertson's the company donates a small percentage of the total sales back to the nonprofit.

Following this pattern is the Dayton Hudson Corporation's fully-owned subsidiary, Target Stores, which helps support K-12 education by giving one percent of qualifying sales purchased on its Target Store credit card to any K-12 school chosen by the cardholder. Such support amounts to millions of dollars each year to eligible schools across the United States.

Exhibit 3.3 shows some of the industries that are good partners for cause-related marketing programs.

An article in the *San Antonio Business Journal* found that "programs in which companies align themselves with the work of charities often help those firms succeed in the marketplace." The *Business Journal* further noted that "a recent advertising industry poll suggested social responsibility was more influential to consumers than paid advertising."

Exhibit 3.3   Examples of Local Industries
That Are Candidates for Cause-Related
Marketing Initiatives

Real Estate Firms
Car Rental Companies
Hotel/Motel Chains
Department Stores
Grocery Stores

SPONSORSHIPS

Another very important source of corporate dollars for the nonprofit sector comes in the form of sponsorships. Sponsorship dollars are sometimes seen by the company as charitable in nature (i.e., tax deductible) or as a marketing or business expense. Sponsorships are one of the easiest sources of funds for a nonprofit to obtain since the company can often approve such requests with little or no paperwork.

The Phoenix-based Best Western International, a chain of independently owned and operated hotels, is an example of a company that actively seeks sponsorships with nonprofit organizations. Exhibit 3.4 shows Best Western's sponsorship policy.

RESEARCH AND DEVELOPMENT FUNDS

Some companies will support nonprofits with research and development funds. This may entail having a nonprofit conduct some kind of research that the company would find useful to increasing sales. For

Exhibit 3.4   **Best Western International Corporate Sponsorship Policy**

Sponsorships must provide:
- Positive company exposure
- Logo placement and/or acknowledgment of corporate sponsorship
- A comparable investment for benefits received

We do consider sponsorships of organizations that:
- Have a conservative, non-controversial mission
- Are fiscally responsible
- Have a nonpartisan outreach
- Are partnered with desirable affiliated sponsors
- Are professional in their conduct in business relationships

Source: Best Western International, Inc. Corporate Sponsorship website.

example, a health agency might be given research funds to determine whether a certain product leads to positive lifestyle changes of those consumers who use the product. Companies underwrite research if they believe the research will help further corporate goals.

Research and development funds tend to be very narrowly focused. It would make more sense for a nonprofit with significant resources and personnel to seek corporate research and development funds rather than a small agency with a strictly localized focus.

SENIOR MANAGEMENT DISCRETIONARY FUNDS

Another source of corporate support comes from senior management discretionary funds. In some companies, senior management has the authority to use corporate funds to provide support to the nonprofit sector. The ability to obtain such funds depends on networking. For the most part information on such funds is not public and policies vary by company. However, some nonprofits may find this to be a viable source of funds, particularly when those companies that have such funds are represented on an agency's board of directors.

CONCLUSION

In this chapter we reviewed the ways that companies provide cash support to the nonprofit sector. Much of this support comes from budgets specifically earmarked as charitable in nature. However, companies also provide a fair amount of cash support from a variety of non-philanthropic budget lines, including marketing and research. In the next chapter we review the sizeable and growing use of in-kind support by companies to help nonprofit agencies.

CHAPTER FOUR

In-Kind Support

In Chapter 3 we focused on ways that companies provide cash support to nonprofit agencies. In this chapter we will focus on the fastest growing area of corporate support of the nonprofit sector: in-kind support.

In-kind support covers virtually every possible way that a company can help a nonprofit agency that does not involve an exchange of dollar-denominated or human currency. At the end of this chapter we will provide a detailed list of some of the ways that companies can provide in-kind support to the nonprofit community.

GROWTH IN IN-KIND SUPPORT

Corporations have discovered that it is possible to help nonprofits with both cash and in-kind support. The Conference Board reported in 1998 that giving by corporations to the nonprofit sector continued to rise but that more of the giving was in the form of in-kind goods and services and that over 25 percent of companies' total support of the nonprofit sector was non-cash in nature. According to the Conference Board, "Non-cash contributions have become an integral component of many companies' contributions and community involvement strategies."

Exhibit 4.1 lists the top ten corporate donors for 1997, based on total non-cash support, as compiled by the Taft Group.

Notice this list's concentration on some of America's largest pharmaceutical companies, which have provided significant amounts of

Exhibit 4.1   Top Ten Non-Cash Corporate Donors in 1997

Company	Total Non-Cash Giving
Merck & Company	$ 157.0 million
Johnson & Johnson	$ 96.9 million
Microsoft Corp.	$ 89.6 million
Pfizer Inc.	$ 82.2 million
Eli Lilly & Co.	$ 72.0 million
IBM Corp.	$ 70.2 million
Intel Corp.	$ 56.0 million
Hewlett-Packard Co.	$ 48.1 million
Bristol-Myers Squibb	$ 30.0 million
Sara Lee Corp.	$ 20.8 million

Source: The Taft Group's Corporate Giving Directory, 20th Edition, 1997.

their product line to overseas health-based charitable relief organizations. Note, too, the inclusion of both IBM and Hewlett-Packard, neither of which appeared on the list of the top ten cash donors noted in the previous chapter. Both of these companies contribute their products, primarily computers, to nonprofit organizations throughout the United States and foreign countries.

COMPANY PRODUCT DONATIONS

As a way to stretch their support of the nonprofit sector, companies have discovered they can help nonprofits by donating, when possible, the products from which the company makes a profit. For example, an airline may be willing to provide unused seats to a nonprofit rather than an outright cash gift. The airline may have empty seats available on specific flights and be willing to release these seats to a nonprofit group, perhaps for a fund-raising silent auction, knowing that the plane will have to fly anyway.

Some sports arenas will sell seats to a nonprofit group at a discount. For example, one Phoenix-based professional sports team promotes "two-fer Tuesdays." Local nonprofits can buy two seats for the price of one and are given permission by the sports franchise to resell both seats to the agency's constituency at full price.

Manufacturing companies also may have excess product available that they may find attractive to donate to a nonprofit. For example, a maker of stereo equipment may find it beneficial to donate an audio system to a cultural organization, particularly at the end of a product life cycle.

CORPORATE TAX BENEFITS

Giving USA reports that, for many companies, product donations are actually more beneficial than making an outright cash gift, due, in large part, to tax benefits provided by the U.S. government. Under current federal guidelines companies are allowed to take as a tax deduction the cost of the product they produce plus one-half the difference between the cost and fair market value. In many cases, this saves the company more in taxes than it would had the company made an actual outright cash contribution.

OTHER IN-KIND CORPORATE SUPPORT

In addition to providing support to nonprofits through donations of items from their product or service lines, companies can also provide a myriad of other non-cash support to the nonprofit sector. We will explore several types of in-kind support in detail and then provide a comprehensive list of in-kind possibilities.

GENERAL OFFICE SUPPLIES

So far, we have only discussed the products that companies make or are in the business of selling. Obviously, in order to make these products, companies spend large sums of money on their infrastructure, including office space, office supplies, and computers, to name just a few, to allow the company to operate. Even products and supplies ancillary to the manufacture of the main product line have a shelf life after which the company will need to either donate, resell, or dispose of the asset.

Nonprofits have found donated office supplies to be useful to their respective causes. Corporations may donate paper, printing items, and computers, among other items. Some companies specifically promote in-kind donations. However, in most companies the donation of office supplies is not a formalized process.

DIVERSITY OF IN-KIND SUPPORT

Examples of in-kind corporate support are about as diverse as one can be imaginative. One of the first, best, and most comprehensive lists of ways that companies can help nonprofits through in-kind contributions was put together in the early 1980s by Alex Plinio, then vice president of contributions for the Prudential Insurance Company. Mr. Plinio's list, as presented in Exhibit 4.2, is as timely today as it was then.

Exhibit 4.2   Examples of Corporate In-Kind Contributions

Employee access
Volunteers
Board members
Publicity help
Financial sources and advice
Legal and tax services and advice
Strategic planning assistance
Market research advice
Printing services
Audio-visual services
Mailing/postage service
Transportation services
Computer and Internet services
Telecommunications services
Loans: Interest-free or below-market rate
Use of company facilities
Rental space and rental give-ups
Energy conservation audits
Internships and career exposure
Use of company art collections

Source: Fund Raising Management Magazine

COSTS OF ACCEPTING IN-KIND GIFTS

While both cash and in-kind support provide much needed resources to a nonprofit agency, there are often costs associated with accepting in-kind gifts that do not occur when support comes strictly in the form of a traditional cash gift.

Even small in-kind gifts may have an implied cost. For example, a company may be willing to donate computers and computer peripherals to an agency. The recipient agency may immediately welcome a gift of this nature, but there are serious questions to be answered. How will the computers be delivered and who will pay for shipping? Who will make sure the computers are in working order? And, once the computers are up and running, who will support them? If a machine malfunctions who is going to make the needed hardware and software repairs and upgrades? In some cases, a nonprofit that desperately needs computers may decide that the risk-reward ratio favors accepting the contribution rather than having to go out and buy new machines. Conversely, it may be wiser not to accept such a gift and to spend limited resources on new equipment.

ENVIRONMENTAL COSTS A CONCERN

Don't overlook the legal and environmental costs associated with an in-kind gift. One college with which the author was associated received an offer to accept an interest in a silver mine with a long history of toxic waste issues. Needless to say, the college did not accept the gift.

Obviously, not all in-kind gifts will have hidden costs associated with them, but those that do will require a full and complete assessment of the costs involved before the gift is accepted.

Exhibit 4.3, which follows, represents a generic gifts-in-kind checklist that an agency could use to determine whether to accept a potential gift-in-kind.

REPORTING AND ACCOUNTING ISSUES

Reporting and accounting issues is another area of in-kind giving that requires careful attention. A common question often asked by both the nonprofit agency and the donor is how the gift will be valued. In most cases, it is common practice for the donor , not the recipient, to assign a value to the gift. In fact, if the donor (in this case, a company) intends to take a charitable gift tax deduction of an in-kind gift valued at $5,000 or more, an appraisal must be conducted. A similar situation would occur if an individual donated a piece of art valued at $5,000 or more to a charity.

A second area of concern may involve how and what type of in-kind gifts should be reported. For example, a company may volunteer to let

---

Exhibit 4.3   Agency Gift-in-Kind Pre-Acceptance Checklist

Name of proposed corporate donor: _____

Description of in-kind gift offered: _____

Describe potential value to the agency:_____

Calculate predicted costs of accepting gift:

   Shipping & transportation: _____

   Personnel time: _____

   Annual maintenance costs: _____

   Legal/environmental costs (if any):_____

   Additional fixed costs such as insurance, if any:_____

   Total predicted costs: _____

Any restrictions placed on the gift by the corporate donor? _____

Based on the above analysis, should agency accept the gift? _____

Agency employees signing off on accepting gift: _____

a nonprofit use the company's conference room, free of charge, for a board meeting. Should the fair rental value of the conference room be recorded as a gift and, if so, should the company receive recognition for the in-kind contribution?

Each agency needs to establish its own written policy on how in-kind gifts will be reported and how this information will be accurately reported to the agency's constituency.

GIFT-IN-KIND REPORTING FORM

When an in-kind gift is received it is important for the nonprofit agency to complete an in-kind gift form and have the donor sign it. This ensures that both parties to the transaction are aware of the gift transaction and that a paper trail exists for the agency's auditors.

An agency should use whatever form it feels comfortable with. Exhibit 4.4 provides an example of a possible gift-in-kind acceptance form.

TIMING ISSUES FOR NON-CASH GIFTS

Nonprofits should watch for and take advantage of companies that are experiencing economic duress. Often the key to asking for a non-cash

---

Exhibit 4.4   Sample Agency Corporate Gift-in-Kind Acceptance Form

Name of corporate donor: _____

Description of item(s) received: _____

Date of contribution: _____

Date items delivered to the agency: _____

Value of gift: $ _____

Who assigned the value? _____

How was value assigned? _____

Company contact person: _____

Title: _____

Address: _____

Phone: _____

Email: _____

Does company want an acknowledgment? _____

Does company want a gift receipt? _____

How will agency log the gift? _____

Where and how will gift be used/housed/located? _____

Will agency provide recognition? _____

If so, how? _____

gift is timing. "Frequently, when the economy starts to do poorly, the first thing that companies want to do is unload excess inventories," which are costly to store and insure, according to Joseph Calabrese, president of the United Way of Rochester, New York in 1998.

The same is also true of corporate mergers when companies need to dispose of excess capacity created by the merger.

CONCLUSION

Every nonprofit needs to incorporate non-cash support into its overall corporate fund-raising strategy. With fully one-quarter of all corporate support now being made in the form of non-cash gifts, it is important for nonprofits to determine the best way to access such support. In-kind support is limited only by the creative imagination of both the donor and the recipient.

While non-cash support can be helpful to nonprofits it is also important to weigh the costs and reporting requirements of accepting such gifts.

A truly effective non-cash gifts fund-raising program will carefully assess the risk-reward ratio of non-cash support and accept only in-kind gifts that will enhance the agency's financial health and augment its stated mission.

In a later chapter we will explore some of the strategies that an agency can employ to significantly increase its in-kind level of support. In Chapter 5 we will explore the third section of corporate contributions: employee volunteers.

CHAPTER FIVE

Corporate Volunteerism

In addition to outright cash support and in-kind support, as reviewed in Chapters 3 and 4, respectively, companies now go to great lengths to encourage employee volunteerism, another viable source of support to the nonprofit community.

XEROX: AN EARLY SUPPORTER OF CORPORATE VOLUNTEERISM

One of the earliest supporters of employee volunteerism is the Xerox Corporation, which initiated a concerted effort to promote employee community involvement in 1971. Called Social Service Leave, the "program reflects Xerox's enduring commitment to the larger community, as well as the deep respect we have for our employees and their commitment to giving something back to their community," according to Xerox Chairman and CEO Paul A. Allaire. Since it launched the Social Service Leave program, Xerox has allowed nearly 500 employees fully paid one-year leaves of absence to volunteer their time on a community project of their choice.

VOLUNTEERISM VIEWED
AS A PRODUCTIVE ACTIVITY

Perhaps corporate America has jumped on the volunteer bandwagon because several recent studies have documented the increase in employee productivity that occurs as a direct result of community volunteer work. Companies are learning that employees who participate in community volunteer programs benefit as much as the neighborhood projects and nonprofit agencies they help. Community volunteer projects give the company the opportunity to connect on a personal level while enhancing the company as a community asset.

One of the pioneers in promoting community volunteer involvement is the Intel Corporation. Intel strongly encourages whole departments within the company to commit to a community project which can occupy as much as a half-day every three months where an employee team spends time together working with a nonprofit agency. Through its Volunteer Matching Grant Program, Intel also donates cash to organizations based on the number of volunteer hours donated by employees.

For its part, the Minneapolis-based General Mills Company matches employee talents and interests to community needs through the company's Volunteer Connection program. In addition, through General Mills' Retirement Plus program, the company's retirees encourage other retirees to engage in volunteer activities in their respective communities.

Corporate community volunteerism has also received a boost from the U.S. government. In April, 1997, in Philadelphia, President Clinton, with the added support and endorsement of several former U.S. presidents, announced a new initiative called "America's Promise," which was launched to encourage companies to promote employee volunteerism in the spirit of helping, in particular, America's young people. As a result of this initiative, hundreds of companies have literally committed thousands of employee volunteer hours to helping American youth.

The Atlanta Business Journal reported in 1998 that the following three distinct, positive advantages develop as an outcome of community volunteer involvement:

1. Employees engage in team-building, which often helps to improve team effectiveness and interpersonal communication

2. Employees briefly step outside of corporate America and become associated with one or more nonprofits that show a commitment to the community

3. Employees have the chance to broaden their skill base by engaging in planning activities that are perhaps quite different than the skill sets they are used to in the corporate sector

MATCH AGENCY NEEDS WITH COMPANY INTERESTS

An agency looking to engage corporate volunteers in a community project must think creatively about the kinds of projects that the agency could make available and then aggressively promote these projects to the head of the community affairs departments of companies in the agency's area.

In an April, 1998 article in the Puget Sound Business Journal, titled "Nonprofits Must Have Smart Marketing Plans," the author looked at the great success that Habitat for Humanity has had in encouraging corporate community involvement. Habitat, which helps to promote home-ownership by using volunteer teams to create low-cost housing developments, has successfully engaged companies and employee volunteers by having company employee teams adopt and build specific homes.

Many of America's largest companies have utilized the skills of their employees to help build homes at various Habitat for Humanity communities throughout the United States. According to the Business Journal article, Habitat has great appeal to corporate volunteer team building because "It's a perfect product (homes for the needy). It offers instant gratification (we see the house rise) and great linkage to the sponsors (banks, building suppliers). It's a wonderful opportunity for employee involvement, and it brings the community together. That's why it is so successful."

From the agency's point of view there are several aspects to an effective corporate volunteer program. Not only must there be an effective recruitment mechanism in place, but the kinds of activities for which you need volunteers and how you will engage these volunteers once they have committed to your cause should be formulated in advance.

One way to do this is to create volunteer job descriptions and responsibilities for areas within the agency for which corporate volunteer support is critical. These job descriptions should be in place before the first corporate volunteer is recruited. Volunteers from the corporate world may expect a demanding job assignment, so be prepared to provide this kind of opportunity.

Exhibit 5.1   Possible Job Assignments for Corporate Volunteers

To assist an agency with its:

Five year strategic plan

Marketing and promotional plan

Annual budget planning

Fund-raising and development program

Board recruitment efforts

Exhibit 5.2   Ways to Recruit Employee Volunteers

Word of mouth

Local publications

Using in-house company volunteer coordinators

Posting notices through Human Resource departments

Contacting local volunteer centers

Utilizing websites run, for example, by ImpactOnline and Energize

Exhibit 5.1 shows some of the jobs that an agency might assign to corporate volunteers.

Exhibit 5.2 provides some methods that an agency may wish to employ to recruit volunteers from the corporate sector.

CONCLUSION

In this chapter we have looked at the growing commitment of American companies to promote and engage in employee volunteerism. Corporations believe that such volunteerism is good for both the nonprofit agencies that are served and for the company since it creates a healthy, positive environment for the employees.

SECTION THREE

The Process

OVERVIEW

In Section One we developed an understanding for the magnitude of American corporate charitable support and its slow, but consistent, annual growth. In Section Two we looked at the ways that companies make gifts to the nonprofit sector. Now, in Section Three, we turn to the process of raising funds from corporations.

In many ways the fund-raising process is similar whether one is approaching individuals or corporations. The process involves five clearly defined, consecutive steps: research, cultivation, solicitation, evaluation, and recognition and stewardship.

A successful fund-raising program incorporates all five steps, sequentially implemented for maximum effectiveness.

We begin our discussion of the fund-raising process with Chapter 6 and a review of the research function.

CHAPTER SIX

Researching Corporate Giving Programs

Now that we have reviewed the ways that companies support the non-profit community, we will look at how to research companies that have charitable support programs. Although there are literally hundreds of thousands of public and private companies in the United States, as well as many foreign companies with United States operations, not all are targets for charitable support, primarily because most companies, like the majority of nonprofit agencies, are quite small and do not have defined charitable giving programs. Fortunately, fairly detailed, comprehensive information is available on America's largest companies and their corporate contributions programs in addition to those of many smaller, regional companies.

Effective research is at the heart of the fund-raising process. No fund-raising program can be truly effective without investigating the charitable giving interests of the corporate sector. As we will see, charitable giving information on some companies is readily available. For others it is not. Information on charitable corporate giving programs can be obtained from directories designed for this purpose, by word of mouth contact with nonprofit sector colleagues, and by calling the company directly.

SOURCES OF RESEARCH INFORMATION ON CORPORATE CHARITY

We will begin our review of the places one can go to research information on corporate philanthropy by looking at directories that are published to provide just such information, followed by less targeted, but still quite valuable, ways to obtain information on corporate giving.

It is important to note the general availability of information on direct corporate giving programs versus corporate foundations. Information on corporate foundations will be much more readily available due in large part to government reporting regulations that surround foundations. Since a foundation is set up with the primary purpose to distribute grants to charitable organizations, it falls under the scrutiny of the Internal Revenue Service. By law, foundations must distribute a minimum of 5 percent of their assets each year and report on their grant activity via IRS Form 990-PF. Since this is public information it is much easier to find and report on the activities of corporate foundations than on direct corporate giving programs.

Published Directories

While several companies publish information on corporate philanthropy, the two leaders in the field today are The Foundation Center, headquartered in New York City and The Taft Group, located in Farmington Hills, Michigan. Both have a number of publications that are specifically designed to help nonprofit agencies identify companies most likely to support their cause.

These organizations, and others like them, charge for this information although it is often available at public and private libraries and nonprofit resource centers in various states. References are made in this chapter to information vendors that a nonprofit agency may wish to contact. Complete contact information appears at the end of this book in the resource bibliography.

The Foundation Center publishes the *National Directory of Corporate Giving*, which is described as "a guide to corporate giving programs and corporate foundations" in the United States. This book has a particularly good bibliography on corporate funding.

The Taft Group produces a number of reference books on corporate philanthropy. Among them are *America's New Foundations*, which provides information on new and emerging private and corporate foundations in the United States, and the *Corporate Giving Yellow Pages*, which lists contact information (names, addresses, and phone numbers) on over 3,000 corporate direct giving programs and company-sponsored foundations. There is also the *Corporate Giving Directory*, noted for its extensive appendices which make it easy to search for information based on factors important to the fund-raising research process. For example, we learned in Section One that companies prefer to give to nonprofit organizations in areas in which the company has operating facilities. Thus, one way to quickly and efficiently produce a list of targeted corporate prospects is to create search parameters that focus on companies that have locations where the nonprofit agency seeking funds is located.

Exhibit 6.1 lists the appendices that are available in the *Corporate Giving Directory*.

Other information vendors provide similar information, but the Taft Group is noted for its thorough and extensive appendices. Such directories help to narrow the universe of all U.S. companies into a much more manageable, workable list of companies. These companies have proven charitable track records and, if approached correctly, may also decide to support your nonprofit agency.

These appendices are quite useful for the process known in the professional fund raising community as webbing. An example of webbing would involve looking at your own agency's board of directors and seeing what other boards, both corporate and nonprofit, they serve on. A directory that lists corporate officers and directors by alma mater, and by corporate, nonprofit, and club affiliation, as the Taft Directory does, would be most helpful for webbing. In this way, one of your board members could solicit a fellow country club member who works

---

Exhibit 6.1   Appendices in the Taft Group's Corporate Giving Directory

Companies listed by

Operating Location
Location of Grant Recipient
Grant Type
Non-monetary Support Type
Recipient Type
Application Deadline

Company Officers and Directors listed by

Name
Place of Birth
Alma Mater
Corporate Affiliation
Nonprofit Affiliation
Club Affiliation

Source: The Taft Group.

for a company with a charitable giving program since this is an obvious link back to your organization.

What might a sample entry look like in a commercially available directory of corporate giving? Exhibit 6.2 provides a hypothetical example using the fictitious Backus Group of Companies.

One can see that the fictional Backus Company is rather enlightened when it comes to corporate philanthropy. Signs of this include the following: the company defers decisions to employee contributions committees in its operating locations (highly decentralized); the company supports an employee matching gifts program to several types of nonprofits (education, arts, and human services); and it encourages employee volunteerism activities through cash incentives. If your agency were to be in one of these operating locations, Backus might be an ideal candidate for support. It is also important to read between the lines. Other than scholarships, Backus is silent on other projects or programs it may provide assistance to.

There are many other sources of information on corporate giving programs than those appearing in commercially available directories designed for this purpose. We will look at a few additional ways to research which companies have charitable giving programs.

Newspapers

Don't overlook national newspapers such as the *New York Times*. On occasion, the Times publishes a special Giving supplement that covers, in part, the giving patterns and interests of some national companies, including Dayton Hudson. The Times, as does the *Los Angeles Times,* also has its own dedicated staff writer who covers philanthropy for the

Exhibit 6.2   Sample Corporate Charitable Giving Information Statement

The Backus Group of Companies, which has operations throughout the United States, believes that education is the key to a trained, effective workforce. The company makes grants to public and private secondary schools in areas where the company's employees live and work. Furthermore, the company believes that it can best leverage its support for programs at schools that work collaboratively.

Support includes direct cash gifts made by employee contributions committees at each of our twenty operating locations. The company also has an employee matching gifts program and will match dollar for dollar an employee's (both full-time and retired) gift to eligible nonprofits in education, the arts, and human services. The company occasionally makes in-kind gifts of office supplies and equipment and encourages its employees to volunteer in the community. The company will provide a $250 grant to any nonprofit where a Backus employee volunteers fifty or more hours in a calendar year. Support is made to scholarship funds. The company does not make gifts to endowment campaigns.

paper. Also, read local and neighborhood newspapers as frequently as possible. Scan for news on corporate charitable contributions found in ads or the Community News section.

Newspaper Advertising

Each year, for example, the Ad Council, a national organization, runs a full-page ad in newspapers across the country indicating the names of corporations and corporate foundations that support the Council's nonprofit outreach efforts. These lists are a valuable source of names of new and rapidly growing corporate donors.

The Chronicle of Philanthropy

Another good source of information is the *Chronicle of Philanthropy*, a national bi-weekly newspaper dedicated to reporting on various aspects of charitable giving both in the United States and abroad. Almost every issue of the Chronicle will include information on selected U.S. companies and their philanthropic interests. For example, the Chronicle, as a regular feature, highlights annual reports of both foundations and corporate foundations. This detailed information often includes an updated status of the featured corporate foundation's current funding interests. On occasion, the Chronicle will run in-depth stories on corporate giving, including statistical information gained from other sources on corporate philanthropy.

Read these stories carefully since the Chronicle will often include quotes from corporate giving officers and directors. Between this, and the Chronicle's regular listing of "Who's New" among grant makers, it is possible to develop and maintain a very accurate contact list of who is presently in charge of corporate giving programs. Printed directories are unable to do this since they are only published, on average, once a year.

The Chronicle also reports on recent grants made by companies and company foundations. Again, this can be valuable information to nonprofits, particularly when the company is located in the same city as the nonprofit seeking funding and it is determined that recent corporate grants have been made to similar nonprofit agencies.

National Newsletters

Another good source of information on corporate giving programs comes in the form of national newsletters to which one can subscribe, or read free of charge in a good public library. Several worthy of note are *Corporate Giving Watch,* by the Taft Group, *The Nonprofit World Funding Alert,* a publication of the Society for Nonprofit Organizations, and *Corporate Philanthropy Report,* from Aspen Publishers.

STATE AND LOCAL RESOURCES

The information presented above represents only several of the national companies and organizations providing comprehensive, in-depth information on companies known to have corporate giving programs. In addition to national organizations there are many organizations at the state and local level that provide information on company giving programs. Many states, including New York, Arizona, and California have guides to corporate giving within those states. Typically, these books are produced by regional or state nonprofit resource centers or private companies. A very good list of these directories appears in the *Non Profit Handbook,* published once a year by the Chronicle of Philanthropy.

In addition to printed resource directories there are many local sources of information on corporate giving, including your local and neighborhood newspapers. For example, the local business news of many communities around the nation is covered by a publication called "The Business Journal." Atlanta, San Francisco, and Phoenix are just three of the many cities that have Business Journals. A complete list of these journals is available at the company's website *http://www.amcity.com.* The Business Journal lists local grants made by companies and local special event benefits supported by the local business community. Another valuable Business Journal tool is the annual "Book of Lists" that each city Business Journal produces on businesses in that geographic area. The Book of Lists will provide detailed contact information on the top 25 businesses in each of a number of business classifications.

Whether it is the Business Journal or your local or neighborhood newspaper, many nonprofits will buy space (or receive donated space) to list their corporate donors. Again, this is a very valuable source of information, particularly for agencies that operate only in a local or regional area.

GENERAL BUSINESS INFORMATION

In addition to research materials designed to appeal specifically to fund raisers there are also many good reference sources for general information on businesses, including company revenues and profit and loss statements. Two good resources are Hoovers, which maintains a website at *www.hoovers.com*, and Wards, which publishes information on private companies in regional directories. Both are available for review free of charge at public libraries with good business resource sections.

THE INTERNET

The Internet is certainly a growing source of information on corporate giving programs and will only continue to grow. Information on select corporate giving programs can be found at The Foundation Center's website *http://www.fdncenter.org*. A number of prospect research offices of colleges and universities have set up free websites that provide a multitude of links to information on corporate giving programs. This information is available free of charge to anyone with access to the Internet. Another interesting site is *http://www.grantscape.com*, a service of Aspen Publishers, which highlights a Funder of the Day. Often this information is about a corporate funder.

CORPORATE AND NONPROFIT ANNUAL REPORTS

Collect annual reports from both companies and nonprofits in your community. Corporate reports will often include information on chari-table giving in a section titled Corporate Community Affairs or Corpo-rate Social Investment. An annual report for a nonprofit will often list companies in town that are supporting that agency. These same com-panies may be in a position to support your agency as well.

Donor Recognition Walls

When visiting a cultural landmark in town that perhaps has recently been refurbished, check for a Wall of Donors. The same holds true when visiting the offices of other nonprofits. These donor walls will typically include the names of local companies that have supported that agency.

Local Business Community

Join the local Chamber of Commerce to receive their membership directory which will have contact information on a multitude of local companies. Keep up-to-date on the local business community. Who is new in town? What businesses are growing? Which companies are increasing market share?

Company Chief Executive Officers

Are you tracking information on company presidents who have a second home in your agency's city even though corporate headquarters and company operations are located elsewhere? CEOs often have the influence to direct gifts to nonprofits even outside of areas in which the company operates. Are you doing the same by communicating with retired company presidents that now live in your agency's city? Former CEOs often maintain clout, particularly in the area of their former company's philanthropic initiatives, for several years after they retire.

Two Percent Clubs

According to Giving USA, most companies with charitable giving programs contribute an average of 1.1 percent of their pre-tax net income to support charitable organizations, but some companies have pledged to contribute 2 percent. A list of these companies, sometimes referred to as 2 Percent Clubs, can be compiled by combing through, for example, Taft Group corporate directories. Also, in cities where this concept is popular, such as Minneapolis, it is usually possible to obtain this information by contacting the local chamber of commerce. One company with such a policy is American United Life Insurance Company. Each year, the company pledges to donate at least two percent of pre-tax income to support charitable organizations.

Research on In-Kind Support

How can a nonprofit increase its amount of in-kind donations? First, do some research. Some of the nationally-based corporate philanthropic research directories on the market today will indicate a company's policy on in-kind donations and, in general categories, what these items are. Also, nonprofit resource centers in some of the country's larger urban areas publish directories of local companies and what these companies are willing to support through in-kind donations.

In addition, two national organizations act as a clearinghouse between corporate America and the nonprofit sector. The Alexandria, Virginia-based Gifts-in-Kind International, and the Northfield, Illinois-based National Association for the Exchange of Industrial Resources, both collect and then disseminate (for a fee) corporate in-kind supplies and materials to nonprofits around the country.

Ask other charities in your area what they have received or query an on-line listserv group on the types of in-kind donations their organizations have received.

If the company has no formal policy on in-kind donations, the best approach would be to contact the company directly and inquire about product donations.

CHECK INFORMATION FOR ACCURACY

Information on corporate giving programs usually comes from two main sources: the company itself, or from commercial for-profit organizations that provide this information for a fee. No matter who provides the information it is important to check it for accuracy and timeliness. Like many things in life, corporate giving programs tend to undergo significant change almost on a yearly basis. A simple way to maintain accurate information is to call the company every six months for an update on current giving policy and guidelines.

PROSPECT RESEARCH DATA COLLECTION

Now that we have reviewed the various sources of information that exist to help conduct effective corporate prospect research, the next step is to record this information in some sort of standard format. Many nonprofits have created a Prospect Research Form to capture this information. Exhibit 6.3 is a sample of what a corporate prospect research form might look like. Note that this information can be put in hardcopy form or maintained in a spreadsheet or computer software program designed for this purpose.

PROSPECT RESEARCH RATING

As you move forward through the research component of the fund-raising process it will become apparent that some companies appear to be better candidates than others for prospective support. Begin to rank these corporate prospects in categories from "most likely" to "least likely" to support your agency.

Exhibit 6.4 is a sample Prospect Rating Form that you may wish to use to help rate companies in your agency's client service area.

Exhibit 6.3 Prospect Research Form

Corporate Prospect Data Record
(Confidential)

Company Name _____

Address _____

City _____ State _____ Zip _____

Company Contact Person _____

Title _____

Telephone _____

Fax Number _____

Email Address _____

Does the company have its own foundation? ____Yes ____No

If yes, name of company foundation _____

General Information:

Company's current funding interests _____

Does company have an Annual Report? ____Yes ____No

If yes, what are the company's funding interests? _____

Limitations and Restrictions _____

Grant Information:

Highest grant company has made _____

Smallest grant company has made _____

Average grant company has made _____

Similar grants made to other organizations:

Date	Amount	Institution	Purpose

Important Dates:

Grant Submission Deadline(s) _____

Company Board Meets _____

Grant Decisions Are Announced _____

Other:

Research Sources Used to Complete this Form:_____

Our Agency's Past Solicitation Record With This Company:

Project	Date	Funded?	Amount

Exhibit 6.4 Prospect Rating Form

Company Name:_____

Rating Characteristic	Company Exhibits This Characteristic?	If Yes, Then Assign This Point Value
Company executive(s) serve(s) on agency's board?	Yes No	10
Company has operating facility in our agency's service area?	Yes No	10
Company has a stated philanthropic giving program?	Yes No	10
Company has already contributed to like causes?	Yes No	10
Company has employees who volunteer with agency?	Yes No	10
Company has employees who utilize our agency's services?	Yes No	<u>10</u>
Total Points Assigned		60

In this example we have created a Prospect Rating Form with a maximum assigned point value of 60. How would we then rate the likelihood that a company would make a gift to our agency? Exhibit 6.5 can be used as a broad indicator of possible support.

Based on this information the development staff should devote most of their time and energies to cultivating and soliciting companies that score more than 40 points. The point scoring system used in Exhibits 6.4 and 6.5 is simply a model that a nonprofit agency may wish to utilize. The number of questions used and the actual points assigned can be modified to more effectively meet a particular agency's personal needs. You may also decide not to provide equal weighting to each

Exhibit 6.5 Likelihood of Corporate Support

Point Score*	Likelihood of Support
51–60	Very High
41–50	High
31–40	Moderate
21–30	Low
11–20	Lower
0–10	Extremely Unlikely

*Based on Exhibit 6.4—Prospect Rating Form.

question. Whatever point system is used, the ultimate goal is to narrow the field of all possible corporate prospects to a select group with both the capacity and propensity to give to your organization.

CONCLUSION

Research is the first, and some would argue the most critical, step in the fund-raising process. You cannot have a successful fund-raising program without first engaging in research. The research needs to be methodical and appropriate if it is to lead to effective and productive fund-raising results. The appropriate use of the Prospect Research Form (Exhibit 6.3) to match agency needs to corporate interests and the ranking of corporate prospects via the Prospect Rating Form (Exhibit 6.4) will assure that only the most likely corporate prospects are cultivated and solicited. This ensures the most productive use of the limited time and resources that most nonprofits can afford to spend on corporate fund raising.

In the next chapter we move to the second step in the fund raising process: cultivation. Just as research is important to identifying the right companies, careful and thoughtful cultivation must take place before the actual solicitation, or ask, can occur.

CHAPTER SEVEN

Cultivation

In the preceding chapter we focused on research, the first step in the fund-raising process. Now we turn to cultivation, the second and perhaps most time consuming phase. A successful corporate fund-raising program will, in large part, be based on the cultivation efforts made prior to the actual solicitation. There is nothing worse than making a cold call on a corporate giving officer and asking for a gift without having done any preliminary cultivation. The same holds true for the few inexperienced nonprofits that still insist on sending a boiler plate proposal to every company in town, knowing in advance that the chance of receiving support is slim at best.

BUILDING RELATIONSHIPS

It is necessary to convince the corporate prospect that they ought to have a business interest in what you are doing and building a stronger relationship. As you study the corporations with which you have relationships, you should ask yourself what you can do that would give the company an advantage in what they are trying to accomplish. This can lead to large contributions.

With this said, there are several cultivation strategies that a nonprofit can employ to increase its chances of receiving corporate support. We will explore some of the strategies that have proven to be useful in the fund-raising community. Far and away, relationship building is the most important cultivation activity that can be employed. We begin with an exploration of ways to build relationships.

ADVISORY BOARDS

A very effective cultivation technique is to recruit local, influential business executives to serve on various advisory boards established by your organization. Some agencies have established separate advisory boards for each project or program in which the agency is engaged. This is done not only to provide expert advice in any number of areas but to recruit as many community leaders as possible.

One question often asked is how do nonprofits identify and solicit prospective advisory council members? First, try to determine the type of person who could provide the best advice on a specific agency program. Then, approach local company human resource or community affairs directors and ask for their help in identifying appropriate corporate volunteers. Many companies have launched corporate community involvement initiatives and now routinely help to match employee interests with agency needs. A very small number of companies have gone so far as to hire a director of corporate volunteerism to help place employees in nonprofit agencies.

Now, the Internet has made the job of recruiting volunteers much easier and much more effective. Whether your agency advertises advisory council volunteer activities at your own website or one of the dozen or more national websites that have been set up for this purpose (such as *www.volunteermatch.com*), many tech literate executives can be recruited in this fashion.

THE RISING STAR THEORY

Another way to cultivate long-term relationships with selected companies is to utilize the rising star theory—calling on corporate executives and querying them on who they believe will, within a given period of time, perhaps five years, rise through the corporate ranks to senior or executive vice president or above. After you have targeted these rising stars, work to recruit these individuals to your agency's advisory councils or board of directors.

Then, somewhere down the road, if all goes according to plan, these mid-level executives will rise to the top of the corporate ladder where they will then be in a position to direct corporate resources in your agency's direction.

CORPORATE CONSULTANTS

Does anyone in your agency (or the spouse of an agency employee) serve as a consultant to corporations? These are relationships that you can build on. Examples are college faculty who consult for companies in the local business community, and museum curators who are asked to consult for art collections of local businesses.

CORPORATE FACT-FINDING VISIT

After relationship building, which can be a long-term activity, several face-to-face visits can be arranged as the cultivation process progresses toward solicitation. The first is the corporate fact-finding visit. Someone from the nonprofit agency, typically from the development department, arranges for a fact-finding visit to the offices of the company's corporate giving director. This visit takes place during the cultivation phase of the fund-raising process. Items discovered about the company's giving philosophy during this visit are then used to shape a more tailored solicitation plan.

As part of the fact-finding visit, see if you can obtain referrals from the company's corporate giving representative. Ask this individual to suggest other companies that may be interested in your agency and if he or she would make a call of introduction to his or her peers or colleagues in these recommended companies.

A corporate fact-finding visit provides the ideal opportunity to put a face to the corporation and to learn more about the company's giving program that cannot be determined by the brief overviews that appear in printed directories. In Exhibit 7.1 we examine some of the questions that can be covered in a face-to-face, non-solicitation interview. In the event that a face-to-face visit just cannot be arranged, a phone conversation, while not ideal, will usually uncover the same information.

ON-SITE VISITS

The reverse of a successful face-to-face cultivation fact-finding visit, where the agency comes to the funder, is an on-site visit, where the

Exhibit 7.1 Cultivation Fact-Finding Visit Checklist

How many people run the corporate giving function?

Can a proposal be hand delivered?

Have the company's giving priorities shifted in recent months?

Is the company interested in supporting nonprofits that work together to solve a common problem?

What procedure should we follow if we wish to submit a grant proposal?

What ideas, from our shopping list of funding priorities, might be of interest to the company?

funder visits the agency. Arranging for an on site-visit by corporate representatives to the agency during the cultivation phase is one of the most effective methods of obtaining corporate support. This takes a lot of time and effort, particularly in an era when business executives are more pressed for time than ever.

Nevertheless, it is well worth the effort to arrange an on-site visit. Informal studies have shown that an agency that includes an on-site visit as part of its cultivation and solicitation efforts substantially increases the likelihood of receiving a corporate gift. Obviously, corporate personnel are able to see your organization first-hand, which gives you a tangible, physical presence that just is not possible through the written word. Now, with the advent of the Internet and streaming video, it is possible to arrange a virtual site visit in the event that a face-to-face visit is just not feasible.

CONTACT REPORT

Just as it was important in the research phase of the fund-raising process to keep thorough and accurate records so, too, is it important to keep a record of all cultivation contacts for several reasons. They provide written, chronological, and factual histories of all contacts, whether written or verbal, that have been made with a prospective corporate funder, and they help keep track of where the agency is in its MOVES cultivation efforts, which we will discuss in a moment.

Exhibit 7.2 is a sample of a contact report form, or call report, that should be filled out each time contact is made with a corporate prospect. This is just one sample of a contact report form for development and fund raising. The form you develop for your agency will really depend on what works for you. The important thing is to become disciplined to generate such a contact report each and every time a con-

Exhibit 7.2   Sample Corporate Contact Report Form
___

Company Name: ABC Company

What kind of contact was made?

(if written, attach correspondence)

   _X_ Letter

   _____ Email

   _____ Phone Call

   _____ In Person

What was the purpose of the contact?

   _X_ Informational

   _____ Cultivation

   _____ Solicitation

   _____ Stewardship/Donor Relations

Describe details of the contact:

A letter was sent to ABC's director of corporate contributions on March 1. The letter, which was signed by the agency's board president, included a copy of the agency's most recent annual report.

Date of Contact Report: March 5

This report created by: The Director of Development

Copies of this report sent to: _____ File _____Others:_____

                                                     (specify)
___

tact is made. By doing so you develop a complete and thorough history of contacts with this potential funder.

So far in this chapter we have discussed a number of ways that a nonprofit can cultivate corporate prospects. We also discussed the importance of keeping good records. How, then, will we know the time has come to move to the third phase of the fund-raising process, solicitation?

To help determine this shift from cultivation to solicitation, many agencies engage in a concept known as the MOVES principle.

THE MOVES PRINCIPLE

Fund raisers rely on cultivating individuals in an orderly, sequential manner. This same format also works for corporate cultivation and solicitation. One popular method employs the MOVES principle, a proven step method that assigns a numerical value to certain tasks. Higher point values are assigned to activities that are more personal, such as a face-to-face visit.

Exhibit 7.3   Assigning Point Values to Cultivation Activities

Activity	Point Value Assigned
Thank You Letter Sent	5
Email Update	5
Phone Call	10
Invitation to Special Event	10
Personal Visit	20

For example, your agency may decide to assign point values to essential cultivation activities as shown in Exhibit 7.3. Next, your agency's fund-raising leadership agrees that a company that accumulates, say, 100 points, within a six-month period is ready to be solicited for a gift. The points attached to each activity and the time horizon used will depend on the agency, its available resources, and its fund-raising needs.

The form shown below, Exhibit 7.4, can be used for each corporate prospect. The form will take up as many pages as the number of cultivation activities required to reach the point threshold that will trigger a solicitation.

CONCLUSION

Like research, cultivation must receive a high priority from the nonprofit agency. A successful solicitation almost never occurs without sequential, strategic cultivation. The best cultivation involves relationship nurturing and building. Such cultivation works most effectively when the agency can develop and maintain human links between the

Exhibit 7.4   MOVES Prospect Activity Form

Company Prospect:_____

Date Cultivation Commenced:_____

Cultivation Activity	Activity Completed?		Point Value Assigned
_____	Yes	No	_____
_____	Yes	No	_____
_____	Yes	No	_____
	Cumulative Point Value:		_____
Ready for solicitation?	Yes	No	

agency and the corporate prospect. The amount of cultivation required will vary by the prospect. A rational, methodical way to determine how much cultivation is needed prior to solicitation is to employ the MOVES principle discussed in this chapter. Cultivation is the prelude to solicitation. In the next chapter we will explore the actual solicitation phase of the fund-raising process.

CHAPTER EIGHT

Solicitation

In any effective corporate development program there comes a critically important time in your agency's fund-raising strategy when you cross the line from cultivation to solicitation. Ideally, just as in fund raising with individuals, it is best to try to have a face-to-face meeting with a representative from the company from which you are seeking support. This is especially true when dealing with major gifts, which are usually large, single opportunity grants for a specific agency program or when your agency is involved in a capital campaign.

In essence, there are two important components to the solicitation phase of the fund-raising process: the proposal and the ask.

THE PROPOSAL

Whether or not you expect to engage in face-to-face solicitation or will be relying on a third person intermediary, such as the agency's executive director or board president, a written proposal is critical to success in trying to obtain direct corporate support. The same is even more true when a face-to-face presentation is just not possible or feasible. A proposal is less critical when seeking support from non-charitable corporate budgets such as marketing and public relations.

Exhibit 8.1   Comparing Private Foundation and Corporate Proposals

	Private Foundations	*Companies/Corporate Foundations*
Proposal Attributes		
Length	Longer	Shorter
Budget Information	Extensive	Brief
Support Documents	Many	Few
Writing Style	Elaborate	Concise

Fortunately, proposals are much simpler in design and length for companies than those required by private grant making foundations. While there is no exact rule of thumb, and everyone who writes proposals has their own personal view on this subject, it is safe to say that most corporate proposals need only be one or two pages in length.

Exhibit 8.1 compares attributes likely to be found in private foundation proposals and proposals sent to companies and their corporate foundations.

One of the more simple and succinct descriptions on how long a corporate proposal should be, and what to include, comes from guidelines written by the UPS Foundation. Exhibit 8.2 shows what the UPS Foundation requires of agencies seeking the Foundation's support.

Although every company and company foundation has its own proposal format, the items required by the UPS Foundation very succinctly state what UPS requires in a letter proposal. Pay particular attention to the last item in Exhibit 8.2. Inexperienced grantwriters often feel it is impolite to request a specific amount. Instead, they will include words such as whatever the company can afford. It is very much to your

Exhibit 8.2   UPS Foundation's Grant Proposal Specifications

Grant Proposal Elements

Qualified organizations seeking grants are encouraged to submit a proposal in concise letter form, not more than two pages in length that contains the following items:

Description and mission of the organization

Description of the specific program/project for which funding is requested

Statement of program/project need and goals

Description of how program/project goals will be attained and evaluated

Total costs of the program/project

List of committed alternate funding sources and dollar amounts for the program/project

Total amount requested from The UPS Foundation

advantage to state a specific funding amount. After all, companies are in the business of working with numbers and budgets and need to know how much your agency is requesting.

Exhibit 8.3 shows a fictional one-page letter proposal that an agency has prepared for a corporate foundation prospect. Usually, a letter proposal should not exceed two pages.

Exhibit 8.3   Sample One-Page Letter Proposal

Mr. Edward Jones
Executive Director
The Backus Company Foundation
559 West 42nd Street
New York, NY 10021

Dear Mr. Jones:

It is a sincere pleasure for the ABC Agency to write to you today. ABC, whose mission is to find ways to bring technology to underserved populations, seeks a grant of $25,000 from the Backus Company Foundation to help us extend our outreach activities.

As you know, ABC is located in one of the cities where Backus has a large operating facility. In fact, many Backus employees live very close to areas where ABC has made inroads to the groups we serve.

Backus has a long and distinguished record of corporate philanthropy in ABC's headquarters location. We very much value the support that Backus has provided to other nonprofits that help disadvantaged populations and hope that Backus will be in a position to help ABC bring its strength in technology education and training to this same group.

We know that program evaluation is a major concern of Backus. We believe that a grant in the amount requested will allow us to set up a classroom with fifty workstations. Our previous work in a neighboring city shows that we can expect to train approximately 25 people each week and, over an eight week period, adequately train over 150 people in basic office skills.

We wish to thank Backus in advance for its consideration of our proposal and hope that it will be acted upon favorably. If you feel it is appropriate we would be happy to have a local Backus representative visit our facility. In addition, the support documents you requested are attached.

Sincerely,

Mary Smith
Executive Director
ABC Agency

Proposal Delivery

When submitting a proposal by mail be sure to send it return receipt requested. This ensures that the proposal is received by the funding source and can also be used to verify that the proposal was received prior to a grant application deadline. Some people believe that a proposal may be seen as more important by the prospective funder if it is hand delivered. If this is allowed, and the agency's resources can afford this expense, then by all means have the proposal hand delivered. Be sure to write "hand delivered" both on the outer delivery envelope and at the top of the actual letter proposal.

THE PROPOSAL ITSELF

Begin with a Strong Opening Statement

When writing a grant proposal try to say everything you have to say in as succinct a fashion as possible within the first two paragraphs. Then, elaborate on the details in later paragraphs. It is often the job of a funder's staff to condense each proposal that is received into one or two paragraphs. These condensed statements (not the full proposals) are then forwarded to the funder's entire board for discussion and possible approval. This is why it is very important to summarize your proposal at the start of the letter, perhaps in the form of an executive summary. Many times this is all the funding board will ever see, so the summary needs to be clear and compelling.

Line Spacing

It is acceptable to single space a letter proposal to a corporate funder unless otherwise instructed because a corporate proposal is often presented in as business-like and professional a manner as possible. Thus, the same format as a business letter is appropriate.

Shopping List of Ideas

A very effective technique is to include a shopping list of funding ideas in the proposal. This gives the funder some choice and prevents them from closing the door on a single project request. A shopping list also allows the funder the opportunity to creatively suggest possible alternatives that might be a combination of some of the agency's needs and one that is of particular interest to the funder. Such a list opens the door for a corporate response that could potentially lead to funding for a totally new project not referenced in the original proposal.

The Funding Mix

As we discussed in Section Two, companies prefer to look at a wide range of funding possibilities and to present a funding package that includes a mix of cash support, in-kind support, and employee volunteers. If an agency predicts this kind of response and presents a proposal that requests several types of funding possibilities, this technique may be very effective.

For example, instead of making a request for a $100,000 grant the proposal might read as follows: a request for a $40,000 cash grant, $25,000 in equipment, and 250 hours of employee volunteer time to help implement the project.

ADDITIONAL DOCUMENTS

In addition to the one- or two-page letter proposal, the funder will often ask for supporting materials that often include one or more of the following items:

The agency's:
- Current budget
- Annual report
- Audited financial statements
- (Copy of) IRS 501(c)(3) designation letter
- Mission Statement
- List of officers and board members and their business affiliations
- List of recent major donors, both corporate and foundation, received in the last twelve months
- Biographical/professional data on key agency staff
- Project/program job descriptions
- Press releases about the program and/or organization
- Letters of endorsement from other agencies
- Statistical data and needs assessment information
- Copy of the agency's IRS Form 990

The support documents required by a potential corporate prospect will vary by funder, but it is important to have these items readily available in case the funder requires them. A complete sample grant proposal which includes all of these support documents appears in Appendix A.

FILING SYSTEM

Before the first grant application is submitted, take time to set up a simple filing system. Multiple copies of each of the items listed above should be made and placed in separate folders in an easily retrievable area. Then, when you are preparing to deliver or mail a proposal to the funder you can quickly pull the requested items from the file (or add as an attachment to email for on-line grant applications). This avoids having to hunt for these items each time a proposal is submitted and having to ask the agency's in-house staff repeatedly for the same information.

Proposal Packaging

Avoid the temptation to use fancy proposal packaging. What really counts is how persuasive your proposal is, not how attractively it was assembled or packaged.

In this computerized age much of what you send (again, unless you do it yourself via on-line grant applications) is simply rekeyed by foundation personnel into grant management and tracking software where the written word takes precedence.

THE ASK

So far in this chapter we have discussed the look and feel of the written proposal. We will now talk about the actual ask and provide some advice for both the corporate fund-raising novice and the seasoned practitioner.

Consider Multi-Year Pledges

However the actual ask is made, whether in letter form or via a personal solicitation, be sure to state a specific dollar amount. Consider

Exhibit 8.4　Pledge Payment Schedule

Gift Amount	Annual Payment	Quarterly Payment	Monthly Payment
$150,000	$ 30,000	$ 7,500	$ 2,500
$125,000	$ 25,000	$ 6,250	$ 2,083
$100,000	$ 20,000	$ 5,000	$ 1,666

asking for a pledge to be paid over a two- to three-year period. Some companies may prefer this option and in so doing make a total gift commitment that would be larger than if the company made a single, one-time grant. It is also important to keep in mind the time value of money, especially if a funder seeks to stretch out payments for a project that your agency will need to pay for today.

Exhibit 8.4 shows a pledge payment schedule developed by the Honolulu-based Kapiolani Medical Center for Women and Children.

The data in Exhibit 8.4 was used by Kapiolani Medical Center for its high end donors during the Center's Working Wonders capital campaign. Note how a $100,000 gift seems much more reasonable when positioned as a gift of $5,000 paid each quarter for five years. Note, too, that the lowest gift option presented is $100,000, thus raising the corporate donor's sights.

Face-to-Face Solicitation

Face-to-face solicitations are best if at all possible. Here are some ideas to use in a face-to-face solicitation that involve the actual ask. First, be sure to have enough copies of the proposal for everyone in the room. This makes it easy for everyone involved to turn to a specific page of the proposal as it is referred to at the meeting or if the prospective funder has specific questions.

Second, consider the number of people making the solicitation. Experience has shown that it is more effective to have at least one additional person representing the agency than the number represented by the funder. Thus, if there is one person in the room representing the funder, the nonprofit agency should have two representatives, perhaps the executive director and the president of the board of directors.

Once the agency is ready to make the solicitation, the following clearance form, presented in Exhibit 8.5, can be prepared.

Exhibit 8.5   Solicitation Clearance Form

Name of Company Being Solicited _____

Company Representative(s) to be solicited _____

Representative(s) title(s) _____

Phone number(s) _____

Email address(es) _____

Date to be solicited_____

Approach: ____In Person ____By Mail

If, in person:

Time of appointment _____

Location _____

Strategy*: ___One on one ___Two on one ___Other

Solicitation clearance approved by:

Agency's Development Director _____

Agency's Executive Director_____

*Number of individuals representing the agency compared to the number of individuals representing the prospective corporate funder.

Overcoming Objections

As with any solicitation, the possibility exists that the funder will raise objections as to why they are not in a position to support the agency. Your solicitors need to be trained to overcome objections and to offer alternative scenarios. For example, a corporate funder may say the request is too large. The solicitors could suggest that the company consider half the amount now with a pledge to be paid out over three years, during which the company's fortunes are expected to increase. Another objection may be that the company does not want to fully fund an endowment. The agency could suggest that the company fund the annual expense of what the endowment is seeking to accomplish for the first three years. The company is then able to fully fund a smaller commitment and the agency is able to pay the annual expenses for three years, during which time another funder may step in with the needed endowment principal.

CONCLUSION

In this chapter we have reviewed the most critical part of the fund-raising process, the solicitation. We could never be successful in raising needed corporate resources for our agencies if we failed to solicit our corporate prospects. All the planning in the world is for naught if we don't follow through with the solicitation. In this chapter we looked at the importance of a well-written proposal, and the proposal attachments that the funder may request. We also discussed the importance of the ask and provided some strategies for a more effective ask. In the next chapter we move to the fourth phase of the fund-raising process, evaluation.

CHAPTER NINE

Evaluation

In this chapter and the following one, we will look at the next three stages of the fund-raising process: evaluation, recognition, and stewardship. Exhibit 9.1 provides a chart of what the post-solicitation fund-raising process looks like.

No matter what the outcome is, thank the prospective funder immediately. Then, evaluate the entire process. The word evaluation can have several meanings in fund raising and we will explore in depth in this chapter the various ways that evaluation is important both to the funding community and to the agency that is seeking support.

There are three types of evaluation in the fund-raising process: solicitation evaluation, project evaluation, and fund-raising evaluation. They are very different but each is very important to the fund-raising process and to the success or failure of an agency's fund-raising efforts.

TYPE 1: SOLICITATION EVALUATION

We will begin with a review and analysis of what is commonly called solicitation evaluation: how effectively did the agency solicit a particular company and what can be learned from this solicitation so that future corporate solicitations can be improved?

Exhibit 9.1   The Post-Solicitation Fund-Raising Process

The Ask Is Made (Solicitation)	
The Funder Makes a Decision	
The Outcome Is	
Positive	Negative
Thank	Thank
Evaluate	Evaluate
Recognize	Strategize
Stewardship	Plan
Begin cultivation for next solicitation	

First, review the funder's response to our request. Was the outcome positive or negative? Did we receive funding or was the proposal declined? If the proposal was declined what, if any, were the reasons the funder provided?

Solicitation Outcome: Positive

Assume, for a moment, that the proposal we submitted was funded. First, break out the party favors, and celebrate! Then, take some time to reflect and evaluate your success. If you are new to corporate fund raising, was it beginner's luck or did you develop a solid solicitation strategy that can be successfully replicated with other corporate funders?

Exhibit 9.2 represents a checklist to determine why the solicitation resulted in a positive outcome.

Exhibit 9.2   Reasons Why Proposals Are Funded

- The proposal was clear and well written
- The request was within the company's guidelines
- The company has previously supported similar projects
- The amount asked for was acceptable by the company
- The company has employees and/or an operating location in the agency's service area
- The agency has people who are connected to the company
- Other_____

(add your own reasons)

Solicitation Outcome: Negative

In a perfect world, every proposal submitted by every agency would be successfully funded. Sadly, the likelihood that a proposal will be funded is typically well shy of 100 percent.

However, we can learn a great deal when a proposal is declined that will help us correct errors and create future proposals that are much more likely to be funded. It is certainly nothing to be ashamed of if a proposal is declined. Companies, like individuals, receive more requests than they could ever hope to fund and are forced to decline some very worthy requests.

Just as we reviewed the reasons why a proposal was funded, Exhibit 9.3 lists reasons why a proposal request may be declined. It is certainly allowed, in fact even encouraged, to contact the funder to inquire why the proposal was not funded. Sometimes it is simply a matter of timing, in which case the funder will ask you to wait until the next funding cycle. Sometimes the funder will allow you to resubmit the request after making some minor modifications. It is not uncommon for a corporate funder to impose policies which limit or restrict the frequency with which a proposal can be submitted. Many companies have written guidelines that state that an agency may not approach the company with a new request until some preset amount of time has passed, typically a year, from the time the last request was funded or rejected.

Exhibit 9.3   Common Reasons Why Proposals Are Not Funded

- The project has not been properly documented.
- The project does not strike the reviewer as significant.
- The funding guidelines were not followed.
- The evaluation procedure is unclear or inadequate.
- The project's objectives are outside the interests of the company.
- The proposal is poorly worded, unclear, or hard to understand.
- The project does not show collaboration with other similar agencies.
- The project is too ambitious based on the agency's resources.
- There is insufficient evidence that the project can sustain itself beyond the life of the grant.
- The proposal budget is not within the range of the company's normal support parameters.
- The company does not know the capabilities of the agency submitting the proposal.

Exhibit 9.4 Solicitation Evaluation Questions

- Was the solicitation made?
- Was the quality of the solicitation good?
- Was the timing of the solicitation appropriate?
- Was appropriate feedback provided by the solicitor?
- Did the solicitor feel comfortable with the assignment?

EXAMINING THE SOLICITATION

We have just analyzed reasons why a proposal may or may not be funded. Next, we will explore the solicitation itself. Exhibit 9.4 provides a list of questions to help evaluate the solicitation process.

CREATING A MORE EFFECTIVE SOLICITATION PROCESS

Now that we have looked at some of the main reasons why a proposal may be turned down, we should look at how we can increase our chances of receiving funding in the future. The worksheet shown in Exhibit 9.5 can be used by an agency to analyze any weak component of the solicitation process and then offer strategies to correct or eliminate the weakness. The worksheet is simply a tool which can be changed or modified to meet the needs of a particular agency's fundraising process.

These are but a few examples of taking a perceived weakness in the solicitation process and looking at specific ways to address the problem. As noted earlier, each agency will have its own set of solicitation strengths and weaknesses and therefore each agency will want to develop its own solicitation strategy improvement process.

The goal, of course, is to develop a more effective corporate solicitation strategy and to continuously look for ways to improve the solicitation evaluation process which, in turn, will lead to more proposals being successfully funded.

Exhibit 9.6 shows an example of the number of proposals successfully funded when evaluation is incorporated into the fund-raising process.

Exhibit 9.5 Examples of Strategies to Address and Correct Weak Solicitations

Identified Solicitation Weakness	Strategies to Improve Process
Proposal poorly worded	Hire outside consultant to write effective proposal copy.
	Have several outside people act as mock-reviewers prior to submitting the proposal.
Proposal outside the funding interests of the company	Review agency's internal research process. How was this company identified? Develop new screening process to filter out companies that do not fund agency's needs.
Proposal does not show collaboration with other similar agencies	Research all local agencies providing similar services. Contact these agencies prior to submission of a grant request and identify possible collaborative efforts.
Volunteer solicitor did not follow through or made poor presentation	Review volunteer solicitation process. Develop more effective volunteer solicitor training program. Determine if paid staff should make solicitation.
(Add one or more solicitation weaknesses specific to your agency)	(What are ways to overcome or mitigate these weaknesses?)

TYPE 2: PROJECT EVALUATION

The second type of evaluation, one that continues to grow in importance, is commonly called project evaluation. This type of evaluation generally is focused on how the agency will evaluate the success, or failure, of the project for which they are seeking corporate support. Setting up this type of evaluation is often a prerequisite of receiving a grant from any funder.

Project evaluation was first mentioned in Chapter 8 as one of the key elements to be included in the text of the proposal. This is often the

Exhibit 9.6 Comparing Solicitation with and without Evaluation

	Old Model – No Evaluation	New Model – Evaluation (Continuous Improvement Process)
Proposals Generated	100	100
Proposals Funded	10	25
Percentage of Proposals Funded	10%	25%

weakest part of a proposal, and, yet, it is becoming increasingly important in the eyes of the funding community. Just as companies must be accountable to their shareholders, they also want nonprofits to be equally accountable to the company by asking the nonprofit how the project funded will be evaluated.

A Brief Historical Perspective on Project Evaluation

The amount of weighting that project evaluation receives in a proposal was negligible 20 years ago. Today, though, it is close to being the most critical aspect of a proposal.

Exhibit 9.7 shows the hypothetical weighting that a corporate funder may give to various elements of a grant proposal.

In an earlier period of philanthropy most funders did not make the development of a project evaluation and reporting procedure a condition of the funding process. Most companies were quite content simply to provide support to local nonprofit groups offering services in areas in which the companies operated.

Two critical turning points or defining moments in the history of philanthropy have thrown a spotlight on evaluation. First is the degree to which company shareholders have taken an interest in corporate affairs. In an era in which there is an increasing focus on all corporate budgets, funders need to justify every expenditure and show shareholders that the company's money was well invested. There is nothing worse than having a company make a significant gift to a nonprofit only to discover later that the agency was forced to close its doors.

In today's world, corporate philanthropy can be better justified if the nonprofit agency is asked to develop and supply an evaluation plan to show how the company's gift was effectively utilized. Thus, we have seen a shift toward the inclusion of a request for an evaluation plan in the written proposal guidelines of a growing number of corporate funders and for that matter, private foundation funders as well.

Exhibit 9.7   Weighting of Grant Proposal Elements

Proposal Elements	1970s	1990s & Beyond
Amount Requested	50%	30%
Project Funded	50%	40%
Evaluation Required	0%	30%
Total	100%	100%

Such a request, which leads to the second major turning point in philanthropy, also forces the nonprofit agency to be more responsive and accountable for how a company's funds are used. As a result of several large national scandals that rocked the nonprofit sector, and received wide media coverage in the 1990s, there has been increasing pressure to make certain that grant funds are used for their intended purpose.

There has been much discussion in the nonprofit community about the impact of these changes in the grant-seeking process. Some agencies have found the evaluation process has become so time consuming and burdensome that the costs of obtaining a grant can, at times, seem to outweigh the benefits.

Fortunately, at least for most corporate gifts, the evaluation process is less onerous than that imposed by the private grantmaking community. For this reason, nonprofits should not be deterred from approaching companies that present a suitable funding match.

Exhibit 9.8 provides a review of the level and cost of providing evaluation by funding entity.

Develop A Solid, Realistic Evaluation Plan

Considering the funding community's level of interest in project evaluation, it is important in the solicitation process to devote sufficient time and energy to developing a solid, specific, and realistic plan on how the project will be evaluated and how best to present this plan to the funder. Oftentimes, this can be accomplished by focusing on concrete, quantifiable information and statistics.

The following is an example of an agency that is trying to increase the number of clients it will be able to serve with the help of a corporate gift. Here are two ways that the agency might word the proposed evaluation plan in the proposal:

Exhibit 9.8   Level of Agency Evaluation Expense by Grantmaking Entity

Funding Type	Amount and Cost of Project Evaluation Required
Individuals	(Typically) None
Direct Corporate Giving	Low
Corporate Foundations	Moderate
Private Foundations	High
Government Funding	Extremely High

1. Example of vague, poorly defined project evaluation plan:

    Our agency knows the importance of your company's val-
    ued support and we welcome the opportunity to work with
    you in evaluating the success of this grant, if funded. We will
    prepare an evaluation for you to show how the company's gift
    made a difference in the number of clients we were able to
    serve.

2. Example of well worded, well developed project evaluation plan:

    Our agency will keep a daily log on the number of clients that
    utilize our services as a result of this grant and will compare this
    to client usage prior to the grant. Our projections suggest that
    usage will climb by 20 percent within three months of deploy-
    ment of the grant and will exceed 50 percent within six months.
    We will provide the company with a month by month usage
    comparison report with cumulative year to date changes over a
    two year period.

Communication—Informing Agency Personnel of Evaluation Commitment

It is also important for the agency's fund-raising staff to keep lines of
communication open with all agency personnel who will ultimately
have to engage in, and be responsible for, project evaluation activities.
Many times the fund-raising staff will be more concerned with raising
dollars than with post-grant evaluation reports. Nonetheless, since post-
grant reporting is such a vital part of the total fund-raising process, it is
critical that all affected agency project staff are aware of the implications
should a grant be awarded.

Summarizing Project Evaluation

There is no doubt that project evaluation, as part of the solicitation
process, has grown in importance over the past decade and will continue to grow. Agencies need to weigh the cost of evaluation as they prepare proposals and solicitation strategies. For example, an agency may
feel it is important to include the tangible and hard dollar cost of meeting evaluation requirements as part of the total grant request. However,
this can result in a Catch-22 situation.

While many funders require project evaluation they do not want
their grant funds to be used for evaluation but rather to be put to work

exclusively for the program or project for which funds were originally sought. Thus, it becomes increasingly important to an agency to determine the costs and benefits associated with submitting a proposal with high-end evaluation requirements.

The decision might be reached to focus only on corporate funders with either no or low-end evaluation requirements. Again, the appropriate strategy to employ will be different for each agency depending on its attitude toward evaluation and the amount of time and expense it is willing to commit to evaluation as compared to the benefits received.

For example, an agency might create a set of solicitation guidelines that only targets corporate gifts where the cost of evaluation totals less than 5 percent of the total grant request. If project evaluation and post-grant reporting procedures will exceed 5 percent, the agency will either not approach the company or request that the company significantly reduce its evaluation requirements. See Exhibit 9.9 for a sample formula that would help an agency decide whether to pursue a grant based on evaluation costs. It is more important than ever for an agency to build into its solicitation procedure the time and expense that funders often require in the post-grant project evaluation process.

TYPE 3: FUND-RAISING EVALUATION

The third type of evaluation has to do with the agency's total fund-raising budget and the most effective allocation of these, quite often, limited resources. It is a very good idea for an agency to evaluate, at least once a year, the effectiveness of the agency's overall fund-raising efforts and to reallocate resources as needed.

What exactly do we mean by this? Let's say that in the first year of an agency's fund-raising program the development budget is allocated in equal amounts to direct mail, planned gifts, and corporate fund raising. At the end of the first year it is determined that as a percentage of

Exhibit 9.9 Decision-Making Formula on Maximum Allowable Evaluation Costs (Sample)

Amount requested:	$ 100,000
Projected amount agency will spend on evaluation:	$ 6,000
Evaluation as a percentage of total grant:	6%
Agency's maximum allowable evaluation expenditure:	5%
Proceed with Grant Request?	No

the cost per dollar raised, corporate fund raising is more cost effective than either direct mail or planned giving. An effective strategy would be to reallocate, in year two, a greater percentage of the fund-raising budget to corporate solicitations. If the reverse holds true, the amount of funds spent on corporate solicitation should be reallocated to those areas that show more promise to the agency. See Exhibit 9.10 for a sample allocation of an agency's funds.

The same evaluation can also be focused specifically on the corporate fund-raising component of the agency's total fund-raising plan. For example, an agency may have implemented a strategy to obtain corporate gifts in the following four areas: tables sold to corporations for special events, in-kind contributions, sponsorships, and cause-related marketing initiatives.

An analysis of the corporate fund-raising program at the end of an agency's fiscal year may reveal that the most productive type of corporate gift was in-kind contributions. If such a finding surfaced as part of an ongoing evaluation process it would be logical to conclude that the agency would want to reallocate fund-raising personnel and resources toward obtaining a wider array of in-kind gifts and reduce resources targeted at, say, sponsorships.

CONCLUSION

There is no doubt that evaluation in all of its different meanings is very important to the fund-raising process. It has also been one of the most overlooked and underrated areas in fund raising. However, the importance of effective, quantifiable evaluation continues to grow in significance not only because it is required by more and more funders but also because it helps an agency to refine and refocus its fund-raising priorities.

Exhibit 9.10   Sample Dollar Allocation of Agency's Fund-Raising Resources

	Pre-Evaluation Allocation	Post-Evaluation Allocation
Direct Mail	25%	20%
Special Events	40%	30%
Major Gifts	20%	25%
Corporate Gifts	15%	25%
Totals	100%	100%

Those agencies that develop well crafted, thoughtful evaluation procedures will be much more likely to succeed in obtaining charitable gifts not only from the corporate community but from all segments of the philanthropic marketplace.

Now that we have reviewed evaluation in all its myriad forms, we will move on to recognition and stewardship, the highlights of our next chapter and the final two components of the fund-raising process.

CHAPTER TEN

Recognition and Stewardship

RECOGNITION

After a company provides your organization with a gift, it is very important to thank all parties involved, including both the volunteer solicitors (if any were involved) and the company, including perhaps the president and the director of community affairs. In 1982, a monthly newsletter called The FRI Monthly Portfolio (now published by the Taft Group) ran a brief article on ways to follow-up with a corporate gift. The following ideas, excerpted from that article and suggested by William Hallstead, then Director of Development at the Maryland Center for Public Broadcasting, are presented in Exhibit 10.1.

The forms of recognition are limited only by the creativity of the organization and can include ideas such as the following:

- A plaque, recognizing the company's support, which is presented to the company during a public ceremony
- Photos, placed in various publications, showing a copy of an oversized check being presented to the agency
- Printing an annual honor roll of donors which lists all of the agency's annual contributors including corporate donors
- Producing and providing press releases on a particularly significant grant
- Listing donors at the agency's website

Exhibit 10.1　Post-Grant Public Relations Ideas

Invite corporate officers to visit your facility to say thank you

Provide the company with an ad in your agency's newsletter

Make sure the company's publication editor is sent an article about the gift

Send formally printed announcements of the gift to a list supplied by the donor

Print up cards and posters describing the gift and give them to the company to use in-house

Recognition and the Media

A good way to recognize a company for its support is to have the company's gift listed in various local media publications which will be very happy to list a corporate gift. For example, the Phoenix Business Journal, a publication of American Cities, includes a Grants and Benefits page in each weekly issue and encourages local charities to submit information on recent gifts and grants.

Recognition in Your Community

Think about recognition ideas you have seen used in your community. Donor walls are very popular in some nonprofit organizations, while others, such as the Boy Scouts of America, hold dinners to thank their corporate donors.

STEWARDSHIP

Perhaps the most overlooked aspect of the grant solicitation process is stewardship. Essentially, this is both the end and beginning of the cultivation process. Stewardship is the process of keeping a donor involved in the organization after the gift has been made. While few in number, some nonprofits have hired individuals whose sole job is to provide effective and sustainable stewardship of donors between solicitations.

In the past decade, nonprofits have begun to seriously embrace the importance of stewardship in all types of fund-raising activities, whether they are aimed at individuals or corporations. Stewardship, or donor relations, is so important that the National Society of Fund Raising Executives (NSFRE) devotes over 10 percent of all questions on its Certified Fund Raising Executive exam to stewardship concerns and issues.

Exhibit 10.2 lists the eight standards of effective stewardship as defined by NSFRE.

Exhibit 10.2   Effective Stewardship Standards as Defined by NSFRE

1. Report to relevant constituents the sources and uses of funds expended and investments managed by the institution to accomplish its mission in order to create confidence in financial operations.
2. Prepare fund-raising reports by gathering appropriate information in order to assure quality decision making.
3. Prepare and recommend to the board policies to ensure that the public's best interest is achieved in the fund development process.
4. Communicate with the organization's leadership to ensure that the organization's values, mission, vision, and program are relevant to the community and invite donor response.
5. Promote a culture of philanthropy to key stakeholders in order to help them understand the organization and the philanthropic and fund development process.
6. Clarify, monitor, and implement the donor's instructions by ensuring that expenditures are appropriate and documented in the organization's financial records.
7. Communicate the organization's position to appropriate constituencies regarding issues that affect the people it serves and the organization's ability to provide services in order to maximize benefits to those served.
8. Comply with pertinent government regulations and procedures by filing reports that demonstrate public accountability.

Source: The Certified Fund Raising Executive Candidate Handbook, published by the CFRE Professional Certification Board, revised 10/97, available through NSFRE.

Customizing Your Own Stewardship Plan

An agency's corporate stewardship program will depend on the time, resources, and personnel available to engage in stewardship activities.

Exhibit 10.3 is a sample of three levels of stewardship that might be appropriate for an agency. Again, the exact level that an agency chooses and what it will include at each level is something that the agency's fund raisers and leaders will decide as a group.

CONCLUSION

Often overlooked, but also a key to the fund-raising process, is the ability to appropriately and effectively thank the donor and then follow this up with stewardship. Stewardship activities are very important since they set the stage for beginning the fund-raising process all over again.

Over the last five chapters (Section Three), we have taken a close look at the total corporate fund-raising process. We began with an exploration of the research function so essential in determining what companies are likely to support an agency. Following research, we

Exhibit 10.3   Levels and Examples of Stewardship Activities

Basic Level Low cost, easy to implement ideas:

1. Send agency's annual report to past corporate donors
2. Send agency's annual executive director's letter to past corporate donors
3. Call corporate giving directors and invite to agency's annual special event.

Intermediate Level Moderate cost ideas:

1. Agency's development director arranges for once a year luncheon with past corporate donors.

Advanced Level High cost, time-intensive ideas:

1. Invite past corporate donors to annual agency luncheon hosted by the executive director.
2. Hand deliver agency's annual report to past corporate donors and include a handwritten note from the agency's executive director.

explored effective cultivation activities, how to conduct a solicitation, how to incorporate evaluation into the fund-raising process and, finally, ways to recognize and steward the donor.

In the next section, we will look at the people behind the corporate funding programs, the key decision makers.

The People

OVERVIEW

For the most part, this book has focused the majority of its attention on the five-step process of obtaining corporate support. However, even the best process will ultimately fail without adding the human element to the equation. You will hear over and over that fund raising is a "people business" and it is not the author's intention to suggest otherwise.

In Section Four we will spend time looking at the many individuals in the corporate sector that can become your allies in attracting support for your agency. These individuals range from the CEO of a small company in your city to, in very large organizations, highly evolved corporate contributions committees consisting of a cross section of employees.

We will learn that the secret to effective fund raising is to engage these individuals wherever possible in your agency's operations. This might simply be an educational process or inviting corporate representatives to serve in volunteer positions.

Let's turn, then, to the role of the decision makers in the corporate giving process.

CHAPTER ELEVEN

The Decision Makers

A book on corporate giving would not be complete without a discussion of those individuals within a company who have the authority to approve support for nonprofit agencies. In the final analysis, no matter how good you are with proposals or research, fund raising is ultimately a people business and it is people who make the decisions. Hence, the more you know about the people in charge and how to approach them, the more likely you are to receive support.

In this chapter we will look at the wide range of people within a company who have control over either corporate philanthropic budgets or other budgets that can be used to support the nonprofit sector. We will begin with a review of the people behind the philanthropic budgets and then move to those people who control other non-philanthropic budget lines.

POINTS OF ENTRY

First, though, let's take a look at the number of points of entry into a corporation as compared to approaching individual and private foundation prospects. One important and positive benefit of companies, at least to the fund-raising community, is the large number of doors, or points of entry, that can be accessed. Compare this to raising funds from individuals or private foundations as shown in Exhibit 11.1.

Exhibit 11.1   Points of Entry by Funding Entity

Funding Entity	Number of Entry Doors	Available Options If Door Closes
Foundations	One	No option*
Individuals	One	No option*
Companies	Many	Move to next door

*After a suitable waiting period, cultivation and solicitation would begin anew.

This chart simply points out that if you were to approach a company for a gift and be turned down you should not immediately give up any hope of support. Simply move to another door, or budget center, within the company. If you approach a company's foundation for a gift and are declined, there is no reason why you cannot go to the company's marketing department to explore a cause-related marketing initiative.

Now, let's look at those individuals who control philanthropic funds at companies.

CORPORATE FOUNDATIONS

Corporate foundations usually have their own dedicated staff who make decisions on their own or in conjunction with the CEO and/or the board of directors of the company. Individuals in charge of corporate foundations often have titles such as president or executive director. The ability to make funding decisions is, in part, restricted by the foundation's written interests and guidelines. Giving is structured and procedures need to be followed, so in some cases, months can go by before a decision is reached.

Typically, requests for funds are directed to the paid head of the foundation. This individual may be entrusted to make the funding decisions alone or in conjunction with other corporate officers.

In this case, the best avenue to pursue would be to cultivate this individual to the extent that time allows. If this is not possible, the next best approach would be to develop a relationship with another officer of the foundation or receive an endorsement of your proposal from a high ranking officer of the company.

Protocol in such a structured environment is quite important so it is best to follow procedures and work within the system. A proposal should be directed to the head of the corporate foundation and not to others in the company who perhaps appear to have the clout or authority to make funding decisions. By circumventing the system, you can ruffle feathers and risk losing funding for an otherwise worthy proposal.

DIRECT CORPORATE GIVING

Direct corporate giving is less structured than corporate foundation support and is, therefore, much more flexible. For this reason, some people in the corporate giving field foresee a possible decline in the number of corporate foundations in the United States in favor of an increase in direct corporate giving programs.

Direct corporate giving is much more spontaneous. Gifts may literally be approved the day the request is received. Conversely, some companies with direct giving programs will only make decisions once a month, a quarter, or sometimes less frequently.

Direct corporate giving programs are often administered or housed in a company's public relations or community affairs department and staffed by individuals with titles such as vice president for public relations or community affairs director, to name but two. These people usually have a number of other responsibilities besides corporate giving. Their ability to make grant decisions on their own is limited. Even in the largest companies, the CEO or founder is often involved in the decision making process.

Although there is no set profile of who administers a corporate giving program, studies done by the Conference Board indicate that it is most likely to be a woman who works less than full-time on corporate giving and has either no staff or, at most, one additional support person. An effective cultivation idea would be to routinely invite corporate community affairs directors in your agency's operating location to your agency's functions and email them when you have a new press release or have added additional information to your agency's website.

THE CEO

In smaller organizations, the company chief executive officer (CEO), who is also oftentimes the company founder, is often the individual who makes the decisions on supporting nonprofit organizations. The CEO can, more often then not, quite simply and spontaneously decide to support a specific charity and have a check cut almost immediately.

It would make sense, then, to cultivate CEOs in your agency's location, particularly in small to mid-sized companies where no formal giving program exists and all funding decisions come from the top.

EMPLOYEE CONTRIBUTIONS COMMITTEES

It has become increasingly popular for companies to establish employee contributions committees to make decisions on corporate charitable giving, particularly in operating locations that are outside of the company's headquarters. This trend continues to grow in part because, like corporate matching gifts, it is seen as a more democratic way to make grant decisions because employees are chosen from the company's rank and file and often bring diversity to the decision-making process that companies seek to encourage. Employee contributions committees are used to help disburse the company's philanthropic budget dollars provided either through the company's foundation or via direct corporate giving.

DECENTRALIZED DECISION PROCESS

One of the first companies to move from a centralized to a decentralized pattern of giving was Allstate Insurance. In 1989, Maxine Powell, then head of the Allstate Foundation, orchestrated a restructuring of the foundation's giving program. The foundation boosted its total contributions budget and gave the company's local field offices more say over how to allocate funds to nonprofit organizations. In fact, Allstate put two-thirds of its total grantmaking budget in the hands of local employee contributions committees, far above the 25 percent that most companies reserve for field operations. The reason for this restructuring was simple. Allstate wanted its philanthropy to become much more employee focused and employee driven.

Other companies that rely heavily on employee contributions committees include General Mills, which has 22 committees around the country. The San Francisco-based Charles Schwab Corporation has employee committees at the company's large regional service centers in Denver, Phoenix, Indianapolis, and Orlando, and the Amoco Foundation formed contributions committees at 14 operating locations in the early 1990s.

INVESTIGATE LOCAL COMMITTEES

Try to become knowledgeable about how a company's employee contributions committee works and under what guidelines it operates. Some committees start off the year with a set amount of funds which are expected to last for 12 months.

Create a list of companies in your agency's operating location(s) that make decisions using employee contributions committees. This information can be found in published directories and by doing some word of mouth investigation with your peers in other nonprofit organizations. Where possible, invite members of the contributions committee to visit your agency and perhaps sit on one of your agency's volunteer committees.

TARGET YOUR APPEAL

When soliciting companies where decisions are made by employee contributions committees, be sure to craft your request or proposal to appeal to these employees. This approach may be markedly different from the way that you would approach upper management.

PERSONAL EMPOWERMENT

In some companies, Intel, for example, line managers in certain departments have the authority to approve small grants without consulting anyone else in the company. This is an example of how some forward-thinking companies are streamlining the grant making process and giving managers on the front lines the ability to immediately approve grants, typically up to a certain threshold such as $5,000.

Make a list of companies in your operating location that have managers with the authority to approve grants. Approach these individuals with ideas for funding that not only help your agency but will have some impact on the company's visibility in the community.

CORPORATE GIVING CONSULTANTS

Aside from those individuals who work within a company's corporate giving program there is a tendency for companies to turn to outside corporate giving consultants. These are typically sole proprietors or, in a few cases, firms that specialize in providing advice to companies in such areas as starting a corporate giving program, from reviewing grant requests to actually making grant recommendations.

A good strategy would be to develop and maintain a list of corporate giving (and strategic philanthropy) consultants where your agency operates. Look in the Chronicle of Philanthropy and Foundation News, published by the Council on Foundations, for consultants who advertise their service. Cultivate these individuals by adding them to your mailing and email distribution lists, particularly if you know that they are working with a company that has expressed an interest in supporting agencies such as yours.

PROFESSIONAL GROUPS OF CORPORATE DONORS

Just like any other professional group, corporate giving professionals belong to grantmaking associations and societies at the national, regional, and local level. At the national level there is the Council on Foundations, which holds an annual conference to discuss issues of interest to corporate (and private foundation) grantmakers. At the regional level, a number of corporate giving professionals belong to RAGs, or regional associations of grantmakers. One of the most established and well respected RAGs in the United States is the Minnesota Council on Foundations. A list of RAGs can be found in various publications, including those produced by the Foundation Center in New York.

At the local level, there are various formal and informal groups of corporate grantmakers. For example, in Arizona there is a group called the Valley Contributors Network, comprised of many of the larger (and sometimes not so large) companies in the greater Phoenix metro area. This group convenes on a regular basis to discuss such issues as trends in corporate philanthropy and streamlining the grant solicitation process through use of a standard or universally accepted application form. For example, the Minnesota grantmaking community, working collectively, created the Common Grant Application Form, which allows Minnesota nonprofits to fill out just one application that is accepted by grantmakers throughout the state.

Cultivate These Groups

Inquire and research if your agency's community has a regional association of grantmakers or a locally based professional group of corporate public affairs officials. Then, invite these groups to host one of their upcoming meetings at your agency's site, or volunteer to speak at one of these meetings after carefully researching and preparing a topic of interest to these professionals. In either case, you will provide your agency with some good public relations.

OTHER DECISION MAKERS

So far we have looked at the decision makers who control a company's charitable support. It is important not to overlook the many other decision makers in a company who have control over other budgets such as marketing and public relations, for example.

Marketing Directors

Every company has a marketing director who is always on the lookout to try to increase the visibility of the company to potential customers. A company's vice president for marketing often has the authority, if the arrangement is appropriate, to approve an expense on his or her budget to help a nonprofit agency. Often this is a quid-pro-quo arrangement. The company hopes to obtain some mileage through such venues as a joint advertising campaign.

It would therefore be a wise idea to alert marketing directors in your agency's operating location to some of the agency's upcoming events and publications which could lead to sponsorship opportunities.

Company Purchasing Agents

Who do you turn to in the company when you are looking for corporate in-kind gifts? Consider cultivating and developing a relationship with a company's purchasing manager or buyer. The main responsibility of the procurement department is to buy needed supplies and services at the most competitive price. However, buyers also become involved with the disposal of office supplies as well.

The primary concern of most company employees is generating company revenue, not helping nonprofit organizations. However, these employees will often turn to the company's purchasing department when they need help in disposing of used supplies and equipment. It makes sense to cultivate a relationship with the purchasing department because they are more likely to think of your agency as a possible home for office supplies that have either outlived their usefulness for the company or represent surplus equipment that the company does not need.

In most cities there are chapters of the Tempe, Arizona-based National Association of Purchasing Managers, or NAPM. One cultivation idea would be to make a presentation at a NAPM monthly luncheon meeting and discuss how purchasing managers can assist the nonprofit community through in-kind support.

Or, take a cue from the National Christina Foundation (NCF), a nonprofit that works with purchasing agents to secure used computer donations. NCF refurbishes these machines and provides them to smaller nonprofits that desperately need the equipment.

Another example is the Phoenix-based nonprofit COMPAS, which actively solicits artwork from companies. COMPAS then sells these works of art at auctions and distributes the money raised to various arts organizations in the community. COMPAS often turns to purchasing managers since, again, these individuals are often called upon to dispose of various company assets.

A FINAL WORD ON THE JUDICIAL SYSTEM

A relatively recent phenomenon is the growing interest of the U.S. judicial system to include court ordered corporate gifts to the nonprofit sector as part of an overall civil or criminal awards settlement. For example, in late 1998, the DuPont Corporation was ordered, by a judge, to contribute in excess of $10 million to three Georgia colleges to settle a lawsuit made against the company.

Although judges, as a rule, are not allowed to engage in fund-raising activities due to possible conflicts of interest, there is no reason why a nonprofit cannot inform the judicial community about their mission or activities.

CONCLUSION

In this chapter we reviewed the key decision makers in a company who have the authority to approve corporate support, both philanthropic and otherwise, to nonprofit organizations. Compared to individuals and private foundations, a variety of individuals in a company control the nonprofit support purse strings.

In many companies, where support can come from several budgets, a number of decision makers work independently of each other. The following important points were discussed. Protocol is particularly important when dealing with a corporate foundation, some line managers in major companies are empowered to approve grants up to certain thresholds, and there are many points of entry into a corporation and it is not uncommon to be turned down by one company budget area only to, with persistence, find support through another corporate budget line.

In the end, fund raising is a people business, and knowing who is in charge and how to approach them is often the key to successful resource acquisition.

At this point in the book we have now covered virtually all the main facets of corporate fund raising. To review, we identified the types of corporate support in Section Two, we analyzed the fund-raising process in Section Three, and we reviewed the key decision makers in this section. In Section Five, we are ready to look at how we can use all this information to create an effective strategy and put this all to work in a case study.

The Strategy

Chapter Twelve   Creating and Implementing an Effective and
                        Sustainable Corporate Fund-Raising Strategy

Chapter Thirteen   Matching Gifts: A Case Study

Chapter Fourteen   Issues, Trends, and Technology

OVERVIEW

Throughout the prior sections of this book we have focused on gaining a better understanding of corporate philanthropy, analyzed the types of support that corporations provide, and then reviewed the five critical steps to garnering needed corporate resources.

Now, in Section Five, we bring it all together by discussing the importance of creating and implementing an effective strategy. Without such a strategy, the five steps of corporate fund raising are just that, steps. We need to bring these steps, or building blocks, to life by designing a strategy that is tailored to our specific agency and its available resources.

Section Five will begin with the importance of goal setting, followed by implementation and evaluation of the strategy. This step by step process, if followed, is virtually guaranteed to increase an agency's contributed income no matter what stage of fund raising background the agency currently is in.

Following a discussion of the strategy, we will put this effective tool into action when we analyze, via a case statement, a strategy to significantly increase income from corporate employee matching gift programs.

CHAPTER TWELVE

Creating and Implementing an Effective and Sustainable Corporate Fund-Raising Strategy

Now that we have reviewed the ways in which a company provides support to the nonprofit community and learned about the processes of research, cultivation, and solicitation, we need to craft a corporate fund-raising strategy. This strategy will be different for each nonprofit agency and will be influenced by time, available resources, and the agency's prior success with corporate giving.

This chapter will be devoted to a discussion of the corporate fund-raising strategy. Chapter 13 will provide details of putting the strategy into action through a case study that focuses on matching gifts.

Exhibit 12.1 lists the essential elements of the corporate fund-raising strategy. These same elements will apply whether raising funds for sponsorships, grants, or employee matching gifts.

For the remainder of Chapter 12 we will review each of the components of the corporate fund-raising strategy beginning with goal setting.

Exhibit 12.1 The Corporate Fund-Raising Strategy

Set Achievable Goals
Create and Implement Strategy
Monitor and Review Progress
Redirect Resources as Needed
Monitor and Review Progress
Completion
Evaluate and Plan For New Fiscal Year

GOAL SETTING

In Section Three considerable time was spent on helping nonprofits understand how to research likely corporate prospects. Once you have established a list of the companies that you wish to solicit support from, the next step is to set annual goals. The best way to do this is to set up a simple matrix or chart listing the types of support you will be seeking and goals for each targeted group.

For example, one of your agency's primary needs may be to obtain unrestricted operating support from local companies. Thus, one goal may be to achieve commitments from 10 companies who, combined, contribute $10,000 to your organization within a 12 month period. Another goal may relate to employee matching gifts. Perhaps your research has revealed that, among your agency's constituency, 24 people work for companies with matching gift programs that include support for your type of organization. Therefore, it may be reasonable to set a goal of obtaining matching gift commitments from six of these individuals, or 25 percent of those eligible to have their gifts matched.

Goal setting will depend on a number of variables including past success in each area of corporate fund raising and the length and depth of the agency's past fund-raising efforts. Other variables include the funds available for marketing and solicitation, the time needed to solicit other fund-raising target groups such as foundations and individuals, and variables beyond the scope of the agency, such as the economic environment.

Setting clearly delineated goals on paper helps to translate these goals into a workable format. Exhibit 12.2 shows what a sample goal setting chart might look like for an agency's annual corporate fund-raising initiative on the first day of a new fiscal year. This chart focuses only on donor counts. In addition to monitoring progress based on donor counts, it is equally, if not more important, to establish dollar goals as well. Exhibit 12.3, which uses the same format as Exhibit 12.2,

Exhibit 12.2   Sample Goal Setting Chart (Donor Count)

Agency's Name
Fiscal Year Corporate Fund-Raising Goals & Progress Report
Donor Count Statistics

Target Group	Number of Prospects	Number of Donors*	Number of Donors Year to Date	Percentage Progress Toward Goal
Corporate Foundations	20	10	0	0
Agency Vendors	50	25	0	0
Matching Gifts	24	6	0	0
Corporate Associates**	200	50	0	0
Company Volunteers	100	35***	0	0
Volunteer Gift Matches	100	35	0	0
In-Kind Gifts	40	10****	0	0

*Projected goal

**A corporate annual giving program

***Projected number of volunteers

****Projected number of separate in-kind gifts

looks at corporate dollar fund-raising goals. Again, note that the chart is set up to reflect only goals. No fund-raising income is reported since we are assuming this is the first day of a new fiscal year. Thus, year-to-date figures are set at zero.

Exhibits 12.2 and 12.3 show a hypothetical situation for an agency on the first day of the agency's fiscal year. Reports should then be updated monthly during the year to show progress toward the goal.

CREATE AND IMPLEMENT STRATEGY

After setting realistic, achievable goals the next step is to implement the strategy. This can be done most effectively by creating a written plan of action. Such a plan will list the five steps of the fund-raising process, starting with research, and how the agency plans to achieve its goal.

Exhibit 12.3 Sample Goal Setting Chart (Dollars Raised)

Agency's Name
Fiscal Year Corporate Fund-Raising Goals & Progress Report
Dollar Statistics

Target Group	Dollar Goal	Dollars Raised to Date	Percentage Toward Goal	Comments
Corporate Foundations	$100,000	0	0	None
Agency Vendors	$ 25,000	0	0	None
Matching Gifts	$ 5,000	0	0	None
Corporate Associates	$ 10,000	0	0	None
Volunteer Matches*	$ 5,000	0	0	None
In-Kind Gifts**	$ 5,000	0	0	None
Total Goal	$150,000			

*Dollar value of company gifts to match employee volunteer time and efforts.
**Dollar value of in-kind corporate contributions.

Example: Agency Vendors

Exhibits 12.2 and 12.3 listed specific target groups within the corporate fund-raising sector, one being agency vendors, those companies that provide goods and services to the agency.

It makes sense to consider agency vendors as possible sources of corporate support since they are already very closely linked to the agency. In Exhibit 12.3, the annual goal for agency vendors was set at $25,000.

A written plan for agency vendors might look like Exhibit 12.4. After the annual strategic plan is written, the next step is to implement each phase of the fund-raising process. For example, the first step of our agency vendors' campaign would be to cultivate the vendors and educate them about the agency's mission.

Exhibit 12.4 Written Plan for Approaching Agency Vendors

1. Through *cultivation* inform and educate our vendors about the agency's mission.
2. Send the agency's annual report to all agency vendors.
3. Through *solicitation* stress the need for participation over dollar amount.
4. Through *solicitation* recruit a vendor volunteer to lead fund-raising efforts.
5. Through *recognition* thank all contributing vendors at the annual agency dinner.

MONITOR AND REVIEW PROGRESS

Each quarter, the agency's fund-raising staff should sit down and review all progress charts to keep them up to date. Staff should review the results just like budget analysts review year-to-date profit and loss statements. For example, if we were halfway through the year in our hypothetical vendor campaign it would be logical to assume that we should be approaching the $12,500 mark in contributions (half of the annual targeted goal of $25,000).

REDIRECT RESOURCES

What if we discover, based on our analysis, we are behind on the vendor campaign? Since only half the year is over there is still plenty of time. Agency staff may agree to redirect resources (both human and financial) to focus on the vendor campaign. Perhaps resources can be redirected from another part of the agency's fund-raising campaign that is markedly ahead of schedule.

Alternatively, the agency staff may decide that the original goals, in retrospect, were unrealistic and reduce the dollar goal by some amount.

YEAR-END REPORTING AND ANALYSIS

At the end of the fiscal year agency staff should take time to list their corporate fund-raising accomplishments. Exhibit 12.5 is an example of a year-end report on corporate fund raising that breaks information down into categories that include in-kind gifts and matching gifts received.

Exhibit 12.5 Fiscal Year-End Report on Corporate Fund Raising

Number of proposals submitted during year:_____

Of these, number ____funded ____declined ____pending.

Number of in-kind gifts received:_____ Total value: $_____

Number of matching gifts received:_____ Total value: $_____

Number of cause-related marketing relationships started:_____ Total value: $_____

Number of corporate volunteers recruited:_____ Total value: $_____

Total value of all corporate donations: $_____

Total goal: $_____

Amount above/below goal: $_____

Exhibit 12.6   Questions to Ask When Assessing the Success of a Fund-Raising
Program

- Did we achieve our corporate fund-raising goals? If not, why not?
- How do these results compare to last year?
- In what areas were we successful? Why?
- In what areas did we have challenges? Why?
- How can we improve the process?

As the staff wraps up the fiscal year, time should be set aside to reflect on the overall corporate fund-raising program and to conduct an assessment of the efforts that were expended. Considering the answers to the questions posed in Exhibit 12.6 will lead to a more productive program in the following year.

CONCLUSION

In this chapter we focused on the importance of creating a written, strategic plan for each component of a corporate fund-raising campaign. The plan is based on setting realistic, achievable goals resulting from prior research conducted on the corporate marketplace's ability to provide needed support.

The strategic plan is similar to those that would be used to solicit individuals and for various components of an overall fund-raising program that includes annual support, major gift support, and planned gift support, in addition to our focus, corporate support.

We learned that timely, regular review and analysis of our progress is critical to the success of the strategy because such a review allows the agency to redirect resources to areas in need of additional help.

In Chapter 13 we will examine ways to increase employee matching gifts using the information learned in this chapter.

CHAPTER THIRTEEN

Matching Gifts: A Case Study

ENGAGING THE STRATEGY

Section Five has, up to this point, provided details on establishing and implementing a strategic plan. In this chapter we will take the reader through a case study to show how an effective, orchestrated strategic plan can be successfully implemented. The case study chosen will focus on employee matching gifts.

We first discussed matching gifts in Section Two, including cash support, of which corporate employee matching gifts was one component. Of all companies with matching gift programs, fully 15 percent will now match their employees' gifts to virtually any qualified charitable organization, and the number of companies that are moving to less restrictive matching policies (i.e., will match gifts made to a variety of nonprofit types) continues to grow.

Our goals for this case study will be as follows:

1. State our goal
2. Develop a strategy to meet the goal
3. Implement the strategy by utilizing the five steps of the fundraising process
4. Review and evaluate the strategy

STATE THE GOAL

The goal you choose will depend on your agency's background. For some established agencies the goal may be to find ways to significantly increase the number of employee matching gifts. For others without a track record of obtaining matching gifts, the goal may be to simply find ways to successfully market the availability of matching gifts to the agency's constituency.

For illustrative purposes we will choose a fictional mid-sized non-profit, the ABC Agency, that currently receives 25 matching gifts a year. The agency's development director would like to set a goal of receiving 50 matching gifts within a fiscal year. Thus, for our case study, the goal will be to double the number of matching gifts received.

SET REALISTIC GOALS

It is important to set realistic goals so that the agency can show some sense of accomplishment. In our example, is the goal of doubling the number of matching gifts realistic? We really will not know until we conduct the first step of the fund-raising process, research. Our research results will reveal how many people in the agency's constituency have been identified as being employed by matching gift companies.

STEP ONE: RESEARCH

Of all the types of support that companies with charitable giving programs provide to nonprofit organizations, perhaps the most well-documented is matching gift programs. Several large, national companies and organizations publish detailed information on matching gift programs. Most of this information, while readily available, must be purchased unless you have access to a fairly well-stocked library or neighborhood nonprofit information resource center.

One of the earliest providers of matching gift information sources is CASE, or the Council for the Advancement and Support of Education, headquartered in Washington D.C. CASE, through its Matching Gift Clearinghouse, publishes (both in print and CD-ROM format) thorough and well-researched information on virtually every corporate matching gift program in America.

CASE, however, is not the only matching gifts information provider. It has several competitors in the field including HEP (Higher Education Publications, Inc.) and Blackbaud's (a South Carolina-based firm, known best for its fund development software) *Matchfinder* software which allows users to quickly identify matching gift companies. Like HEP, Blackbaud's database provides current matching gift requirements and ratios for many U.S. companies. HEP is particularly helpful because it lists all of a company's divisions and subsidiaries that are matching gift eligible. Full address and website information on these publishers can be found in the Resource Bibliography at the end of this book.

The vendors you will choose to order from will depend in part on the type of information you need, your budget, and the ease with which you find the information presented. As noted, several vendors allow you to research matching gift programs via their Internet sites although, again, only after paying an annual subscription fee.

Whatever source of information you wish to use, it will be very easy to identify companies located in your agency's community that have matching gift programs. Most companies will match gifts made by their employees no matter where they live or work, even if corporate headquarters is hundreds or thousands of miles away.

Note, too, that many matching gift programs not only match gifts made by current full-time employees but also by current and retired officers and directors, retired employees, and, on occasion, spouses of employees. Each company is different so you will need to check which categories of employees qualify for matching gift support.

In addition, all of the matching gift information vendors mentioned above also provide details on which companies will match gifts based on employee volunteer efforts, to be discussed in more detail later in this chapter.

A sample of this information for the American Express Company, provided at HEP's website appears in Appendix E.

Identifying Your Constituency

Once you have determined which companies in your agency's operating location have matching gift programs you will need to cross-reference this with those in your constituency (whether clients, staff, or friends) that work for these companies. This is why it is so essential to, at every opportunity, ask for employment information. One very easy and popular way to do this is to always ask for business cards at every event or meeting where this is feasible. For example, if you have an open house, be sure to place a fish bowl in a conspicuous location into which people can drop their business cards. You might even go so far as to invest in a luggage tag laminating machine to provide a service to your constituency. Just be sure to keep a second copy of the business card for your records.

You will be amazed at how many people are willing to share their business card with you. Business cards contain a wealth of information, including title, company name, and now, more often then not, email addresses.

Also, make it possible for people to provide you with their business information even if they don't have a business card. Develop a postcard that requests essential business information including, if possible, information on the spouse's employment and whether or not either spouse is retired. Again, it is important to collect spousal employment information as well, since some companies will match gifts made by an employee's spouse.

Retired Employees

It is important not to overlook retired individuals because a fairly large number of companies will match gifts made by retirees. If your agency is located in an area that attracts a significant number of retirees, this is something that you will want to pursue aggressively. Retirees that are receiving defined-benefit retirements (i.e., a fixed amount of income for life) and who own their own homes are often in a position to make larger gifts than current employees who have high monthly living expenses.

Completing the Research: Constituency Analysis

During the research process we cross-referenced employment information on our agency's constituency with those employers that have matching gift programs. The research will usually disclose that a significant number of agency constituents work for matching gift companies and that these individuals are not taking advantage of their employers' matching gift programs for two primary reasons: they do not know about the matching gift program offered by the employer or they are not in the habit of making a personal monetary contribution, which is required before a matching gift can be obtained.

Set The Goals

Based on the analysis of our constituency and how many we have identified as working for matching gift companies, we can now set realistic, workable matching gift fund-raising goals. We will use the same goal setting charts used in Exhibit 12.2 and 12.3. Let us assume that our research for our fictional ABC Agency reveals that 250 individuals in our donor/prospect database work for matching gift companies. We will further assume that we have accurate address information on everyone in the database for both home and business.

The development director of ABC Agency would like to see 50 employee matching gifts made during the year, which translates into a fulfillment rate of 20 percent of all eligible constituency members. Let's further set a dollar goal for matching gifts. Assume the average corporate matching gift to ABC last year was $80. The ABC fund-raising staff would like to increase the average corporate matching gift this year to $100. Exhibit 13.1 displays this information.

Exhibit 13.1 sets the donor and dollar goals for ABC's matching gifts fund-raising efforts for the start of the fiscal year. As the year progresses the appropriate columns will be filled in.

Note that ABC has set the dollar goal higher then the estimated average of $100 per company match. Normally the goal should be $5,000, or 50 gifts at an average of $100 each. ABC, however, has set a goal of $5,500. Why? ABC has noted that several of the agency's constituents work at companies that, in addition to matching cash gifts, will also match gifts based solely on employee volunteerism.

In addition to the 50 prospects that ABC has targeted for financial support, they have also identified two additional constituents who currently volunteer for ABC and work for matching gift companies. ABC anticipates that these two employers will make gifts of $250 each to ABC in recognition of the volunteer activities the companies' employees have provided to the agency.

Once the agency has completed its research and set appropriate goals it is time to implement the strategy. The ABC fund-raising staff will meet as a team and lay out the strategy they will employ. Exhibit 13.2 shows the strategy ABC will engage to meet the goal of obtaining 50 matching gifts during the fiscal year.

Exhibit 13.1 Matching Gifts Goal Setting Chart

ABC Agency				
Fiscal Year Fund-Raising Donor/Dollar Goals Progress Report				
Matching Gifts				
Number of Prospects	*Donor Goal*	*% Goal**	*Donors to Date*	*% Toward Goal**
250	50	20	—	—
Number of Donors	*Dollar Goal*	*% Goal*	*Dollars to Date*	*% Toward Goal*
50	$5,500	100	—	—

*Donors as a percentage of prospects.

Exhibit 13.2   ABC's Strategy to Obtain 50 Corporate Matching Gifts

1. Through *cultivation*, educate and inform our 250 constituency members about the matching gift programs of their respective employers.
2. Include information on matching gifts in all *solicitation* materials and highlight this information to the extent possible.
3. Find ways to make it easy for the constituent to make a gift and to obtain and complete the required matching gift application form.
4. Through *recognition and stewardship* thank the donor as many times as possible.

Now that the written strategy has been completed we can move to step two of the fund-raising process, cultivation.

STEP TWO: CULTIVATION

Once you have determined who in your agency's constituency works for a matching gift company the next step is to make these individuals aware of their employer's matching gift policies. One way to do this is to send out a brochure that lists companies that have matching gift programs. Such a brochure, which fits comfortably into a #10 envelope, is available from CASE. CASE also allows you to buy rights to the information and print your own customized brochure. Another option, growing in popularity, is to create your own brochure which lists perhaps the top 25 or 50 employers in your specific community with matching gift programs.

A number of nonprofit groups are also turning to the Internet to make this information available to their constituency. Many nonprofits now have their own website to promote their services and provide information on their cause. Several have begun to promote matching gifts and allow visitors to their sites to see if their employer will match their gift to the agency.

Other ways to spread the word about matching gift programs include placing reminders in monthly agency newsletters and always inquiring in direct mail, email, and phone solicitations if the individual works for a matching gift company.

Workplace Presentations

Consider taking your agency directly to the workplace. A number of companies will allow an agency to hold an informational seminar for employees in a company conference room during lunch.

Sometimes the agency identifies a member of its constituency who is an employee of the company and asks the employee to host a brown bag lunch with others in the company who are also supportive of the agency. During the presentation a pitch is made to have everyone present consider a gift to the agency and to have it matched by the company.

Everyone in attendance is provided with a company matching gift application form and a pre-addressed reply envelope to forward the form and gift to the nonprofit. This concept is popular with educational institutions with a large concentration of company employees but it will work with almost any type of nonprofit.

During the cultivation phase we seek to inform and educate our constituency about fund-raising gift opportunities. In our case study we have chosen to focus on employee matching gifts. However, the process of informing and educating will be similar no matter what area of fund raising is targeted.

Now let us assume that the staff of the ABC Agency has completed successful cultivation of its matching gift eligible constituents. Perhaps this was accomplished by contacting everyone by letter to let each constituent know they work for a matching gift company. Perhaps the agency held a workplace luncheon information session.

Now that cultivation has taken place ABC can begin the solicitation phase of the strategy.

STEP THREE: SOLICITATION

After we have completed our research and cultivation we need to find effective ways to solicit members of our constituency. We face two major challenges when seeking matching gift contributions. The first challenge is to find ways to encourage our constituency to make their own personal gifts. Since we are focusing on matching gifts in this case study we will assume that ABC's constituency understands the agency's mission and needs and will give, if properly motivated.

MATCHING GIFTS PROVIDE GIVING INCENTIVE

Employer matching gifts can be an incentive in themselves to motivate a person to consider a gift. Here's how: Allow donors to count the company's matching gift towards recognition in one of your agency's gift clubs. Let's say, for example, that an individual makes a gift of $50 to your agency and has it matched by his or her employer on a one-for-one basis. If your organization has established gift club levels, at $100, $250, $500, and $1,000 and has established a policy to allow corporate matching gifts to count, the individual would be recognized at the $100 level of giving even though his or her own personal gift was only $50. With the company's match the total support received by the agency is $100.

How Matching Gifts Work

In most instances the donor is required to send the company's matching gift application with his or her gift to the nonprofit organization. The nonprofit then acknowledges the donor's gift, completes and signs the accompanying matching gift form, and then mails it to the company or to the company's fulfillment service. There are exceptions to this procedure. In some cases, the donor sends the completed application directly to the company. In more and more cases, companies are automating this process by allowing employees to complete a matching gift application via phone. A list of these companies appears in Appendix C.

The second challenge is to motivate our donors to obtain, and later complete, the matching gift form from their respective employer. One of the first ways to encourage matching gifts is to always include information on this important way of giving on any donor contribution response form that the agency publishes.

Exhibit 13.3 shows a donor response form that encourages matching gifts. Notice the proactive approach implied in this donor response card. Donors who are not sure if they work for a matching gift company are encouraged to call the agency for more information.

Exhibit 13.3 Sample Matching Gift Donor Response Form

___Yes, I wish to support the work of the ABC Agency with a gift of $_____.

___My check, made payable to "ABC Agency," is enclosed.

___Please charge my credit card.

___I am employed at _____

My employer ___is* ___is not ___ I don't know, a matching gift company.

*If you are unsure if your company will match your gift please call Ms. Jones at ABC Agency who can assist you in this matter, or you may wish to contact your personnel office for more details.

*My employer's matching gift form is enclosed.

Highlight Matching Gifts in Solicitation Appeals

Prospective donors need to be reminded about matching gift opportunities as often as possible. This includes finding ways to highlight this information in direct mail appeals. One way to do this is to order a supply of CASE's Matching Gift Reminder Notes (Post-it notes on which the message "Check to see if your employer will match your gift!" appears) to include in your agency's written appeal.

As an alternative, you could hand-write your own Post-it notes. These notes are an easy, highly noticeable way to help the reader focus on matching gifts. They can be hand-applied to direct mail appeals and even attached to large direct mail campaigns handled by a mailing house.

ACKNOWLEDGEMENT LETTER REMINDER

Many individuals, for one reason or another, fail to include the matching gift form when they mail in their gift to the organization. Many times this is an oversight. On some occasions this happens because the donor is no longer with the company. When it is an oversight it is a good idea to include a paragraph in the acknowledgement letter stressing the importance of matching gifts and encouraging the donor to obtain and complete the necessary paperwork. For example, at Golden Gate University in San Francisco, all appropriate acknowledgement letters include a statement similar to that shown in Exhibit 13.4.

PREPAID REPLY POSTCARD

Some organizations will take this process one step further by sending the donor a pre-stamped postcard on which the company's address is already printed, with instructions to the donor to sign the back of the

---

Exhibit 13.4 Matching Gift Letter—Donor Reminder

Dear Recent Donor:

Our records indicate that you are presently employed by XYZ Company. Did you know that XYZ will match your recent gift to our organization? You can obtain your company's matching gift form by calling Ms. Jones, the company's matching gift coordinator, at 888–555–1212 or writing to her at corporate headquarters. If for some reason you are no longer with XYZ please drop us a line so that we may update our records.

Sincerely,

The ABC Agency

Exhibit 13.5   Donor Completed Postcard to Send to Employer

Date

Dear Employer:

I recently made a gift to ABC Agency and would like to have XYZ Company match my gift. Please send me a current matching gift application form. My address is _____. Thank You!

Sincerely,

Generous ABC Donor

Note: The employer's mailing address has already been pre-addressed on the reverse side of the postcard by the nonprofit agency.

postcard and mail back to the company. Exhibit 13.5 shows the message on the reverse side.

Some agencies will include a postcard as described in Exhibit 13.5 because most companies will not voluntarily provide a nonprofit with a supply of blank matching gift forms. It is typically corporate policy only to send applications directly to the employee, but some companies will send a supply directly to the agency. If your agency has a relatively large cluster of employees from a single company it would behoove you to inquire directly with the company if they will provide you with blank forms that you can, in turn, distribute to these individuals.

Some companies, such as Intel, allow employees to print the matching gift form off the company's community relations website. A copy of Intel's matching gift form for education is reprinted in Appendix D.

STEP FOUR: EVALUATION

As we have noted before, the fourth step in the fund-raising process is to evaluate our success in the areas of research, cultivation, and solicitation. If we have achieved our goal at this point, then again, everyone has the right to celebrate. If not, what can we correct? Were we correct in our research methodology? Were we really working off an accurate list of members of the agency's extended family who work for matching gift companies? Were we effective in our cultivation strategies? Would it behoove us to do a focus group to see if people recall seeing information about matching gift opportunities? Did we accurately present the opportunity to have an individual's gift matched by their employer? All of these questions would require some analysis and feedback during the evaluation process.

STEP FIVE: RECOGNITION AND STEWARDSHIP

The fifth and final step of the fund-raising process is recognition and stewardship. It is very important to take the time to thank donors who have also taken the time to go through the steps necessary to obtain a matching gift form from their employer and to complete the application.

Thanking Matching Gift Donors

As with any type of fund raising you can never thank the donor enough, and matching gift contributions are certainly no exception. In fact, matching gifts provide an ideal opportunity to thank the individual employee donor twice: once when he or she sends in the original gift with the matching gift application and again when the gift is actually matched by the company.

Exhibits 13.6, 13.7, and 13.8 show some sample notes that your agency may wish to use to thank donors and companies at various stages in the matching gift process.

REVIEWING THE STRATEGY

We have now moved through all five stages of the fund-raising process, from research through solicitation to recognition and stewardship. At this point it would be helpful for the ABC Agency to analyze its strategy to see if it has been successful.

Exhibit 13.6   Sample Note to Thank a Donor Who Has Sent In a Matching Gift Application

---

Dear Friend:

Thank you very much for your recent gift to our agency and for enclosing a completed matching gift form with your contribution. We have verified your gift, signed the matching gift form in the appropriate place, and forwarded it to your employer for processing. We will send you another acknowledgment when we receive the company's matching gift. This process may take some time to complete. Rest assured, however, that we will notify you as soon as the matching gift is received. We value your support and appreciate your company enhancing your personal gift.

Exhibit 13.7   Sample Note to Let the Donor Know You Have Received the
Company's Match

Dear Friend:

It is a pleasure to inform you that our agency has received a matching gift in your
name from XYZ Company. We are most grateful for your part in directing this gift to
our agency, and we thank you for your thoughtfulness.

Exhibit 13.8   Sample Note to Thank the Company for Its Support

Dear Corporate Executive:

It is a sincere pleasure to thank XYZ Company for its recent gift of $X to match the
gift recently made to our agency by your employee, Ms. Jones. We are truly apprecia-
tive that your company has established a matching gift program to benefit nonprofit
organizations like ours. As part of our acknowledgment process, we are also informing
Ms. Jones that we have received your contribution. Thanks for your support!

Let's say that we are nine months into the fiscal year and ABC deter-
mines that the goal it set for matching gifts will not be reached. The
staff has found that 30 gifts have been received and matched. However,
there are still 20 more to be received within three months if this particular goal is to be met.

The staff can address the problem by having quarterly strategic re-
views. In this case, ABC may wish to try the following strategy:

1. Call everyone who is match eligible and ask them to consider a
   gift.
2. Offer an incentive to anyone who sends in a gift with a completed matching gift form within the next 60 days.
3. Recruit team captains at major matching gift employers to encourage employees to give to ABC.

These are just some of the ideas that ABC could try. The important
point is that the staff takes time to review ABC's matching gift goals on
a regular basis. Then, if necessary, adjustments can be made to the
strategy in an attempt to meet the goal on schedule.

ADDITIONAL MATCHING GIFT ISSUES

Up to this point, we have looked at ways to identify, cultivate, solicit,
and thank individuals who work for matching gift companies. Before
we leave this case study we need to turn our attention to some additional issues that affect matching gifts.

Matching Gifts Based on Employee Volunteerism

A discussion on matching gifts would not be complete without mentioning the growing interest of corporate America in providing cash grants to nonprofits based on where the company's employees volunteer their time. One of the pioneers in using matching gifts to promote volunteerism is the Levi Strauss Company. In 1981, then chairman of the company, Walter A. Haas, Jr., announced that Levi Strauss would match gifts to any type of nonprofit agency based on the simple fact that one of Levi's employees volunteered to either serve on a nonprofit's board or to serve in some other volunteer capacity. In this situation, Levi agreed to provide a cash grant, usually in the amount of $500 per agency, even though the employee had not made a cash gift as well, but, rather, had simply volunteered his or her time to a favorite cause.

As an added incentive to motivate employees to serve on nonprofit boards, some companies will also provide matches on a basis greater than one-for-one. For example, the American Express Company will double match a gift made by an employee who also certifies that he or she serves on a nonprofit board. American Express employees who qualify simply check off a box on the company's matching gift form which reads: I have requested the Foundation to double match my contribution to the agency listed. I certify that I serve on the agency's board or have volunteered 50 hours or more during the past 12 months.

Another example of a company that has established a volunteer matching gift program is the San Francisco-based Charles Schwab Corporation Foundation. Termed the A.S.S.E.T.S. Awards Program (or Assisting Society through Schwab Employee Teamwork and Service), this program provides awards to nonprofit organizations with whom Schwab employees actively participate as volunteers.

Schwab's total cash contribution via the A.S.S.E.T.S. Program can be up to $250 to an agency based on a single employee's volunteer efforts to a maximum of $2,500 to an agency in which a Schwab team of four or more employees collectively volunteers 400 hours of service within a 12 month period.

Strong Correlation between Volunteer Matching Gift Program and Company's Long-Term Health

A research study conducted by Arizona State University's Nonprofit Management Institute, in 1999, found a very strong correlation between a company's commitment to making cash grants based on employee volunteerism and the company's long-term health and prosperity. In fact, the study found that companies that have had such programs for ten years or longer actually become the dominant player in their respective industry and, over time, acquire their competitors. The correlation is not nearly as strong when analyzing companies that have opted for a traditional matching gifts program where only cash gifts made by employees are matched.

Applying the Company Matching Gift

Most companies have explicit rules about how the nonprofit is to use the company's matching gift monies. A number of companies require that their gift be applied to the same fund or program to which the employee has contributed, which is more often than not a restricted-use fund. Alternatively, some companies insist that the company match be placed in an agency's unrestricted account no matter how the employee's gift was posted. This can actually be quite good for an agency since raising funds for unrestricted purposes is rather difficult to say the least because most donors prefer to restrict their personal gift to a specific agency project or fund.

If your agency is in need of unrestricted funds, focus your efforts on identifying and motivating employees of matching gift companies that require their match to be unrestricted. Work with these employees to be sure they complete the appropriate matching gift form when sending in a personal gift to your agency.

Timing of Matching Gift Distributions

After the appropriate paperwork is completed and returned, the company will cut checks to the various nonprofit agencies that have submitted applications. The timing of these checks will vary by company policy. Some companies will send checks out continuously, while others will send them on a monthly, quarterly, or even annual basis. With this in mind, it is important for an agency not to depend on corporate matching gifts for immediate income, and therefore to project matching gift cash flow prudently.

Pending Matching Gifts

Create a folder in which you keep copies of all unmatched matching gift forms (those that are still waiting for the company to send its matching gift). This is a good way to stay on top of companies that, for one reason or another, never respond with a gift. By keeping a file of open matches you can work with the companies in question to find out what is slowing down the process. Sometimes you will find that the original form was never received or that the employee was actually ineligible for a match, perhaps because he or she has already hit the ceiling for eligible matching gifts in a fiscal year.

Matching Gift Processing Firms

Some companies, in an effort to reduce costs and streamline repetitive tasks, have outsourced the matching gift fulfillment process to outside firms. For example, American Express utilizes Riverside Software Service Bureau, a New York-based firm. Employees complete their matching gift application, then forward it with their gift to the nonprofit agency, which then, in turn, mails it to the service bureau.

Consider developing a relationship with the matching gift processing companies. Have them add your agency's full name and exact mailing address to their database. Then, when and if an appropriate gift is received and processed, there will be no question about where it is to be mailed.

CONCLUSION

This chapter provided the reader with the opportunity to see, first hand, how to implement a successful fund-raising strategy which can work with any component of a fund-raising program, whether it be major gifts, planned gifts, annual gifts, or, in this case, matching gifts. The principles remain the same.

We learned that there are several components to implementing a successful fund-raising strategy, including setting realistic goals based on research of the constituency, establishing a written plan, using the five steps of the fund-raising process to implement the plan, and, from time to time, assessing the strategy. If need be, the strategy can be modified or adjusted at any time during the fund-raising period in an attempt to achieve the desired results.

In the final chapter we will look at some other issues that face today's corporate fund-raising staff. These include the importance of timing issues, the growth of international corporate philanthropy, and the continued advance of the information age.

CHAPTER FOURTEEN

Issues, Trends, and Technology

Much of this book has focused on the fund-raising process and the implementation of an effective strategic plan. We now turn our attention toward the timing issues that impact the fund-raising process and the strategic plan.

TIMING ISSUES

As you prepare your overall strategy to seek and obtain corporate funding it will be important to be cognizant of timing issues related to the solicitation process. An old axiom in fund raising is that the majority of a fund raiser's efforts in corporate and foundation philanthropy tend to come to fruition only after that individual has moved on to another job. Studies suggest that, on average, the typical development officer will be with the same agency for approximately two to three years. With the long lead times that accompany corporate solicitation requests it is easy to see why this fund-raising axiom may be true.

Companies, foundations, and individuals all respond with different levels of speed to how soon they will respond with a gift to a nonprofit organization. While individuals may be willing to make a gift either on the same day or shortly after they are solicited, companies tend to work on a much longer time frame.

Corporate foundations have even a longer time horizon. A good rule of thumb for a direct corporate giving program is to allow anywhere from three to six months from the time an agency conceives the idea of approaching a company or a company foundation until actual fulfillment of the gift. Corporate foundations can take somewhat longer to make decisions, perhaps six to twelve months. Exhibit 14.1 lists time horizons for different types of donors.

There are three main reasons why corporations and foundations need sufficient time to make their decisions. First, most companies and company foundations have application deadlines and funding schedules that may be as often as once a month or, at the other extreme, once a year. Therefore, if you happen to apply just after a deadline, the wait could be up to a year. Second, many times you will need to do some advance cultivation of a company which, itself, may take several months. Third, even after you do submit a proposal the company may indicate that the project is worthwhile but request that you wait until the next funding cycle so that the company will have sufficient resources to fund your agency's request.

Matching Gifts

The same timing concerns hold true with matching gifts. Most companies will process employee matching gift applications on a monthly, quarterly, or annual basis. Thus, if you forward a completed matching gift application to a company it could conceivably be more than a year before the company sends its match to your agency depending, again, on the company's particular matching cycle and when the matching gift application is received.

If you have a number of donors who make fairly significant annual gifts to your agency and these gifts are eligible to be matched by their employers, be sure to solicit their gifts and complete the matching gift application materials well before the deadline. Many donors forget to complete the matching gift application, so you need to allow sufficient time to remind the donor if this should happen.

Exhibit 14.1   Donor Decision Making Time Horizons

Donor Type	Decision Time Horizon
Individuals	Short, possibly days
Corporations	Mid-range, 3 to 6 months
Corporate Foundations	Long, 6 to 12 months
Foundations	Longer, 12 to 18 months

Cash Flow

Timing issues are important in terms of an agency's cash flow. While a nonprofit should not have to rely on corporate largesse to survive, too many fund raisers and executive directors do not allow sufficient time in their planning and solicitation schedule to accommodate the company's interests and needs. If a short time horizon is all that an agency can afford, it will behoove the fund-raising staff to focus on support from individuals who have the capacity to respond much more quickly than the corporate sector.

Leadership Changes

Unrelated to cash flow, but equally important, is the need to monitor changes in leadership of both corporate foundations and direct corporate giving programs. As much as we would like to believe otherwise, decisions on which agencies receive funding are often based on the personalities of those involved.

Approach corporate funders just after there has been a change of leadership at the top. Many times the new person or group in charge will not have any preconceived funding priorities and will likely be more open to funding any type of program. As the leadership ages, they tend to become more focused on specific types of programs and agencies they wish to support.

Also, keep abreast of newly established corporate foundations or direct corporate giving programs. Sometimes, companies will go out of their way to make a splashy presence in their community by announcing a new giving program. There are also several printed directories on new foundations, for example, The Taft Group's Directory, *America's New Foundations,* which provides detailed information on both new and emerging private and corporate foundations in the United States.

Grant Deadlines and the Funder's Fiscal Year

Almost every direct corporate giving program and virtually all corporate foundations have funding application deadlines. Very few companies review grant requests on an open, ongoing, rolling basis. Also bear in mind that a company's philanthropic budget is usually set in advance and must last for a year. The best time to approach a company is just before or immediately after a new budget year begins. Therefore, it is extremely important to recognize and honor these deadlines.

Too often, an application is submitted just prior to the deadline. It is important to realize that many others are doing exactly the same thing. Proposals received just before a deadline usually do not receive the same thorough review as those received earlier in the application process. If you tend to work best under duress, when you know a deadline is nearing, consider completing the application but then deferring submission until the window opens again in the next funding cycle. This way you not only have a chance to review and refine your agency's proposal but you also have the added visibility of being one of the first applicants to apply in the new cycle.

The odds of receiving funding can be increased by doing complete and thorough research on the funder's interests and how closely they dovetail to what your agency has to offer.

While they may seem minor, timing issues can have a serious impact on an agency's corporate fund-raising program. Agencies need to take into account the speed with which companies react to proposals and not book anticipated income before it is received.

Also, without doing sufficient networking and research, proposals for support may end up being received just after a crucial deadline, forcing the agency to wait up to a year before applying again.

The thoughtful nonprofit will take timing issues into account when formulating a corporate fund-raising strategic plan.

TRENDS

No book on corporate fund raising would be complete without a review of some of the trends facing corporate philanthropy today.

International Corporate Philanthropy

Because of the growing importance and influence of companies with a global rather than national reach, companies with headquarters outside of the United States need to be mentioned. As we move ever closer to a global economy we are seeing an increasing number of foreign companies with a presence in the United States, just as American-based companies extend their reach into foreign markets.

Partly as a way to increase acceptance of their operations in the United States, many foreign-owned companies have made it a high priority to support the communities in which they conduct business, much like our own U.S.-based companies. This area of corporate philanthropy is already so well recognized that the Taft Group produces an annual *Directory of International Corporate Giving in America and Abroad*. As the title implies, the directory focuses on many of the top foreign companies that have operations in the United States, including such well-known names as Honda, Toyota, and Sony, to name just a few. Giving USA[1] reports that fully 80 percent of all Japanese-affiliated companies with operations in the United States engage in corporate philanthropy and have U.S.-based executives that are actively involved in reinvesting their company's funds in U.S. nonprofit organizations.

If your agency is located in a city with foreign-based corporate entities, be sure to include them as prospects in your fund-raising strategy. A good source of information on foreign-owned businesses in your state can be obtained from your state's Department of Commerce. International companies, in particular, want to be seen as good corporate citizens and will often support a wider range of nonprofits than will their U.S. counterparts. As an example, NUMMI (New United Motors and Manufacturing Company, Inc.), a joint venture of General Motors and Toyota, located in northern California, aggressively seeks out corporate community involvement activities that involve both cash gifts and employee volunteerism.

Decentralized Decision Making

There has been a pronounced shift towards decentralizing the corporate giving function, meaning that many companies are moving away from housing all corporate philanthropic decision making at headquarters and allowing more of these decisions to be made at the field office level.

Sometimes this is done to speed up the decision making process. Many companies have chosen to delegate responsibility for nonprofit grant support to employee contributions committees at operating locations.

Decentralized decision making is usually seen as a benefit to nonprofits seeking support, since it brings the decision making down, quite often, to the local level. In this way, it is easier and less costly to network and build relationships with potential funders since the people who make the decisions live in the same area.

Outsourcing

There has been a distinct shift towards outsourcing of corporate philanthropy back office functions including, among others, matching gift processing. Companies have found that it is much more cost effective to delegate certain clerical functions to outside organizations who can handle the same work more efficiently and at a lower cost.

Matching gift fulfillment is a good example. Companies tend to spend an inordinate amount of time processing the paperwork associated with

---

[1]*Source:* Survey of Corporate Philanthropy at Japanese-Affiliated Operations in the U.S.; New York, June, 1995, by the Japan External Trade Organization (JETRO).

matching gifts. In response to this, several companies have been established whose sole product is to process matching gift forms for other companies.

In-Kind Support Increasing Rapidly

As noted in Section Two, there has been marked growth in the volume and value of in-kind support that corporate America is providing to the nonprofit sector. As of 1996, in-kind support represented about 25 percent of all support provided by corporations to nonprofit agencies. This trend is unlikely to diminish any time soon.

Mergers and Acquisitions

Another trend that has been impacting the corporate sector has been the increased merger activity that seems to accompany economic prosperity. Each time a merger is announced, the nonprofit community wonders if the philanthropic support of the merged companies will continue at its current levels or if the new corporate entity's total giving will be less than the sum of the prior two companies. Sometimes there is a drop in giving and sometimes there is not.

Take the recent example of the merger of Regions Financial Corp. and First Commercial Corp., two regional banks located generally in the southern United States. At the time the merger was announced, both banks pledged to set aside a considerable sum of money for a new corporate foundation.

Although most nonprofits feel somewhat threatened by mergers, due to a perceived drop in funding, the numbers prove otherwise. If corporate giving, in the aggregate, continues to increase at close to 6 percent a year, and has done so over a number of years, then mergers must not have such a serious impact as generally assumed.

Part of this is explained by the fact that corporate America is a dynamic landscape. Just as some companies merge, others are spun off. Just look at the phone company. When AT&T was split up, seven regional Baby Bells were created overnight. In addition, the AT&T Foundation was created. It is now one of the largest corporate foundations in America today.

The Corporate Sector's New Aggressive Stance

Interweaving company business objectives with a company's charitable giving seems to be a growing trend. In fact, some companies are demanding that their philanthropy be tied more closely to the products or services they sell. A case in point (although not an isolated one) is the Atlanta-based communications giant, Cox Communications. Nonprofits that approach Cox for a charitable gift are being told with greater frequency that the company will make a gift only after the agency agrees to make Cox the exclusive provider of some of the company's services, such as high-speed-Internet service. This is a trend that must be watched closely and on which further study and research needs to be conducted.

TECHNOLOGY

No one will argue that corporate giving has made a significant impact on our society and because of its importance to the nonprofit sector, more and more information on corporate giving has been made accessible, first through published hard copy directories and now through a new range of information age medium. There is no doubt that the new technologies will impact how we approach companies and how they, in turn, respond to our requests for support. We will now explore some of the ways that nonprofits have learned to use technology to their advantage.

The Internet's Impact on the Corporate Giving Process

The Internet has already had a substantial impact on corporate giving, as it has in so many other areas of our lives. In this section we will look at ways that the Internet is not only helping but changing the way that nonprofits approach companies for support.

One distinctly new trend initiated by corporate funders is to invite nonprofit organizations to submit grant proposals over the Internet. The list of companies that allow agencies to submit on-line grant proposals has been growing exponentially. There are several distinct advantages to on-line grant submissions. No paper is wasted and no postage is spent.

Receipt of the proposal is instantaneous and guaranteed with an immediate email response (sometimes the company will request that certain support documents either be mailed or sent as attachments in email). Finally, the amount of information that an agency can submit is limited to short written text, thus alleviating the expense of fancy cover folders and presentation packets.

A list of current companies that accept on-line grant proposals can be found at a website maintained by Arizona State University's Nonprofit Management Institute at *http://www.asu.edu/xed/npmi/topten*. One such company that permits applying on-line is The Ceridian Corporation. A copy of their on-line grant application appears in Appendix B.

Employee Contributions Committees

As noted earlier, there is definitely growth in the number of companies that leave the decisions on corporate philanthropy to employee contributions committees. Many of the individuals who sit on these committees are tech-savvy, in part because their companies have the resources to create a fully wired technologically advanced corporate climate. These individuals are quite comfortable using email and the Internet.

It would behoove nonprofit organizations to do what they can to utilize the same technology. For example, some companies will allow an agency to submit a two-page proposal as an attachment via email directly to the chair of the employee contributions committee. The chair will then distribute the proposal, or a condensed version of it, via the company's email system to everyone serving on the committee. The committee members then review the proposal and email their recommendations back to the chair.

Be sure to include your agency's website address and place it prominently in the proposal. This allows the reviewer (each member of the employee contributions committee) to click on your website and learn more about your agency. This is an extremely efficient way of distributing information to a select, targeted audience without having to generate any paper. In a constantly expanding global economy when every minute of time is valuable, this allows a reviewer to quickly and effectively obtain an overview of your agency. Thus, you will improve your agency's chance of obtaining a grant if your website provides accurate and timely information in a friendly and easy to use format.

Matching Gifts

Keep in mind that technological advances continue to be made in the area of matching gifts. General Electric, for example, now allows employees to complete matching gift applications by phone. It does not take a great leap of faith to extrapolate this to the Internet. Employees will be able to complete matching gift forms on-line and transmit the form electronically either to the nonprofit or to the company with proof of a donation made via credit card on a secure server.

Obtain corporate matching gift forms and scan them into your agency's computer. Then, post them at your agency's website and encourage members of your constituency to fill out the form on-line while at the same time making an on-line gift by credit card.

Email As a Tool

We are all learning that email can be a very effective tool in communicating with our constituencies. Email, of course, has its limitations but it can also increase the flow of information among a large number of people at a very low cost. In this context, here is an example of how the technology can help with the proposal process.

Most experts recommend that a proposal that is about to be submitted to a prospective funder be routed in advance to all parties in an agency (including the volunteers) that may be impacted by a positive outcome. Sending the proposal out as an attachment to a cover note sent by email is a very efficient, inexpensive, and rapid way of disseminating the information to those involved.

Conversely, email can be a very effective way of alerting the same group when the funder makes its decision, whether it be positive or negative.

Research

The author recently participated in a workshop, sponsored by Arizona State University's Nonprofit Management Institute, titled How To Conduct Superior Prospect Research Without Leaving Your Desk. The advent of the Internet has made such a workshop topic possible. It is now feasible to access all kinds of information, often free of charge, at various websites that provide detailed information on corporate giving. As with any industry, a number of sites provide some free information and charge a fee for more detailed information.

For example, The Foundation Center makes certain information available for free but also charges a fee for more detailed searches. A recent new competitor in the on-line corporate giving information arena is the Phoenix, Arizona-based Oryx Press, which has made available, for an annual fee, a product called GrantSelect which allows the user to search an extensive funding database using a number of different screens or key word searches. Web addresses for both The Foundation Center and Oryx Press can be found in The Resource Bibliography following this chapter.

Another list of references titled *How to Find Funding on the Web* has been produced by Nonprofit World, a publication of the Society for Nonprofit Organizations (see page 56 of Volume 15, Number 6,

November/December 1997). Separately, the Chronicle of Philanthropy printed a page of *Internet Addresses of Foundations and Corporate Grant Makers* on page 34 of their April 18, 1996 issue.

Email Listservs

Many tech-savvy nonprofit fund-raising professionals subscribe to various email listservs that allow people around the country (and around the world for that matter) to post questions and receive responses via email. There are many listservs that are specific to various types of fund raising such as corporate giving. Two of the best sources of information on available listservs are provided by American Philanthropy Review at their website: *www.charitychannel.com/forums* and the Florida-based Nuts and Bolts Information Service which provides an extensive list of nonprofit listservs at *www.nutsbolts.com*.

Computer Software for Grantmakers

A number of companies rely on software to track grant requests and the status of all incoming proposals. Typically, these companies have purchased this tracking and reporting software from an outside company that developed the software. Consider going to a trade show where such software is being promoted. See if you can test-drive the software. Learn the software's limitations and field parameters. Then, fashion your proposal to include key words and phrases that the computer will self-select or which will be manually entered by a keyboard specialist. Title proposals and projects with words that start with A so that when the computer sorts the information your agency and/or its project are always listed first. Study the size of grants that the company makes and be sure to limit your request to the acceptable grant range. In this way, the computer software will not de-select your proposal if it falls outside of normal funding parameters.

Computer Software for Grantseekers

Nonprofits also utilize their own software to monitor and streamline the grant-seeking process. Such software is helpful to keep essential information on prospective funders. Have the computer keep track of corporate funding deadlines and provide staff with an alert both 30 and 60 days prior to a deadline.

Maintain computer records on the types of in-kind support that a company has been known to make. Then, as staff within your agency request specific items, you can cross-reference these with companies in your database and target them for support. You need not spend a lot of money on software as a simple spreadsheet will often suffice.

Subscribe to email services that will alert you to a company's quarterly profits. If they drop precipitously, institute a request for a company's excess inventory which, if received, can be recorded as an in-kind gift.

CONCLUSION

There is no doubt that the information age will have a significant impact on the way that nonprofit agencies approach corporations for support. Some of the latest uses of technology, particularly the growing use and acceptance of the Internet, have been featured in this chapter.

Technology has the power to allow nonprofits to communicate with prospective and current corporate donors more quickly, more often, and more cost effectively. Nonprofits that embrace the technology will be able to maintain their edge in the competitive corporate support environment.

Appendices

Appendix A

SAMPLE CORPORATE PROPOSAL

This appendix is designed to show the reader the contents of a full corporate proposal. As noted earlier in the text, a full corporate proposal is almost always required when submitting a grant request to a corporate foundation and sometimes necessary when submitting a request to a company with a direct corporate giving program.

A model corporate proposal consists of the items outlined in Chapter 8, beginning with a one- or two-page letter proposal, followed by a number of attachments typically required by the funding entity. Please note that this model proposal contains almost every support document that would ever be required. In most instances only one or two of these attachments will normally be requested.

To help the reader more readily understand the necessity of each item in a corporate proposal, the following format has been arranged: As you turn each page a model copy of each document in a proposal will be provided on the right side. The left facing page will contain a description of each model document and when it should be used.

THE LETTER PROPOSAL

This is the main, most important item in a proposal. The letter proposal, normally no more than two pages, should be succinct and tightly written. The ask should be made in the first paragraph and it should be clear and to the point.

Be sure that the letter proposal is written on the agency's letterhead and that the name, address, and salutation of the person to whom the letter is directed is accurate. Also, make it a point to include the name and address of the contact person that you want the company to respond to. Will it be the person signing the letter or someone else within the organization? If the company response will be directed to the agency's executive director rather than the fund-raising staff, make sure the director and his or her immediate staff know that the response should be forwarded to the development and grantwriting staff.

Remember to follow through with any promises made in the proposal. For example, if the proposal says "we will contact you by phone the week of the tenth to discuss this proposal in further detail" be sure that you do exactly that. The company will expect it and not take kindly to those who fail to follow through.

The ABC Nonprofit Agency
1500 York Ave, Suite 1000
New York, NY 10028
(212) 540–9234

Mr. James Able   January 2, 2000
President
The Horton Company Charitable Foundation
595 West 95th Street
New York, NY 10021

Dear Mr. Able:

The ABC Nonprofit Agency seeks the support of the Horton Company Charitable Foundation with a $10,000 gift to be used to help renovate the west wing of our outpatient clinic in lower Manhattan. The ABC Agency is celebrating its 25th anniversary of providing exemplary patient care to indigent New Yorkers by launching the $500,000 "Campaign To Remember," which includes several bricks and mortar projects including the west wing renovation.

The Horton Company Charitable Foundation has been a consistent and faithful supporter of charitable organizations in the New York area since Mr. Horton started the company in 1952. Like so many other nonprofit organizations in New York, we, too, are most grateful for the vision Mr. Horton had for improving the quality of life in the metropolitan area.

When ABC Agency opened the lower Manhattan clinic in 1979 to much fanfare we were able to provide services to over 100 people per week. Over the years the demands for our services have finally outstripped our limited space, which is no longer adequate to meet our long-range objectives and is in severe need of modernization.

We estimate that the total cost of renovating the west wing will be $250,000 which, as you can see, is the main fund-raising project in our capital campaign. To date we have received commitments of $100,000 from two other local foundations and three members of our board.

The Agency certainly hopes that the Foundation will look favorably upon our request. Upon completion of the renovation a wall of donors will be placed in the first floor foyer to permanently recognize those individuals, companies, and foundations that help to make our dream a reality. I will call you next week to discuss this project with you in further detail.

Sincerely,

Abby Johnson
Executive Director

P.S. Please note that I have attached the appropriate support documents noted in your Foundation's guidelines.

AJ:tb
enc.

IRS LETTER OF DETERMINATION

Without fail, every funding entity will require organizations which are to receive funds to provide sufficient evidence that they are, indeed, established as a nonprofit organization. This is typically accomplished by providing a copy of the IRS letter of determination in which the IRS states that the agency in question is set up as a nonprofit.

It would be very hard, if not impossible, for a nonprofit organization requesting charitable support to receive funding without such a letter. Of course, it would be possible to receive non-charitable support, but without the IRS letter these donors could not take their gift as an approved tax deduction.

Internal Revenue Service   Department of the Treasury
District Director   1000 State Street, Anytown, USA

January 1, 1975

Abby Johnson
Director of Financial Operations
The ABC Nonprofit Agency
1500 York Ave, Suite 1000
New York, NY 10028

Dear Sir or Madam:

Our records show that the ABC Nonprofit Agency is exempt from Federal Income Tax under section 501(c)(3) of the Internal Revenue Code. This exemption was granted in December 1974 and remains in full force and effect. Contributions to your organization are deductible in the manner and to the extent provided by section 170 of the code.

We have classified your organization as one that is not a private foundation within the meaning of section 509 (a) of the Internal Revenue Code.

If gross receipts for your organization reach $25,000 or more in any one year, the organization will be required to file Form 990, Return of Organizations Exempt From Income Tax.

This letter may be used to verify your tax-exempt status.

If we may be of further assistance, please contact your local IRS office.

Sincerely,

EP/EO Correspondence Examiner
Customer Service Section

THE BOARD OF DIRECTORS

Attaching a list of the agency's board of directors is an important addendum. The agency's executive director serves at the pleasure of the board, who is ultimately responsible for the success or failure of the nonprofit in question.

While it should not make a difference, some grant requests receive a positive response in part due to the makeup of the board of directors. Having some prominent or influential board members that are recognized in charitable circles can, on occasion, have a beneficial effect on the grant seeking process.

It is a judgment call as to how much information to provide to a funder regarding board members, for example, their addresses and phone numbers. Some agencies will provide detailed contact information including the names and email addresses of each board member's assistant and information on each board member's spouse. However, this happens only in rare circumstances.

Regardless of the degree of information included, a roster of the agency's board should include, at a minimum, the board member's name, company affiliation and title, if any, and perhaps the city in which they live.

The ABC Nonprofit Agency
1500 York Avenue, Suite 1000
New York, NY 10028

The Board of Directors

Chair:
Mr. Robert Ashworth
Chairman & CEO
Ridgeway Industries
New York, NY

Vice-Chair:
Mrs. Claire Letts
VP, Marketing
The Alger Group
Newark, NJ

Treasurer:
Mr. Lyle Farber
Sr. Vice President
Hope Manufacturing Company
New York, NY

Secretary:
Ms. Cynthia Ramirez
Owner
The Pampered Pet
New York, NY

At-Large:
Mrs. Margaret Hightower
President & CEO (Retired)
The Matrix Organization
Bal Harbour, Florida

Mr. Oscar Depworth
Private Investor
New York, NY

Mr. Keith Cooper
Executive Vice President
NetPlanet.com
New York, NY

THE AGENCY'S BUDGET

Most proposals submitted to a potential corporate funder will include the organization's annual budget for at least the past year. Sometimes funders will ask for comparable figures over a longer period, say the last two, three, or five fiscal years.

This information is important to the funder because it helps determine the financial health of the organization. Is the agency in the red each year? Is the situation improving or worsening? While many nonprofits turn to funders to help them regain a shaky footing, the general rule of thumb is that funders want to help make strong organizations stronger.

The agency's budget should be laid out in a simple-to-read format that reflects an accurate picture of the agency's financial affairs. Funders have an uncanny ability to read between the lines and look for weaknesses that can sometimes be used as a reason not to fund an otherwise worthy proposal.

The ABC Nonprofit Agency
1500 York Avenue, Suite 1000
New York, NY 10028

The Budget for Calendar Year 2000

Revenues:

Client Fees	$ 50,000
Product Sales	$ 25,000
Federal Grants	$100,000
State of New York	$ 50,000
City of New York	$ 12,000
Yorktown Development Group	$ 18,000
Donations	$250,000
Total Projected Revenues	$505,000

Expenses:

Administrative	$125,000
Client Services	$175,000
Physical Plant	$100,000
Insurance	$ 10,000
Payroll Taxes	$ 25,000
Thrift Shop	$ 50,000
Total Projected Expenses	$485,000
Anticipated Year-End Surplus	$ 20,000

AUDITED FINANCIAL STATEMENTS

For most corporate funders, particularly the big corporate foundations, the inclusion of a projected budget put together by the agency's fiscal officer is not enough. The funder will also typically require that an annual audit be conducted by a qualified outside accounting firm. Only very occasionally will a funder allow a grant to be made to a nonprofit that produces unaudited financial statements.

The reason is simple. Corporate funders want to ensure that the agency's needs are real and that the agency's financial affairs are in order. While an outside audit cannot completely assure that there is no fraud, such an audit usually provides an accurate indicator of an agency's financial condition.

We are not going to produce the actual audited financial statements here. If you are the fund raiser for your organization, simply obtain copies of the most current audited financial statements from the agency's finance office.

The opposite page contains a sample cover letter that an accounting firm will typically include as a preface to the audited financial statements.

Phillips, Corcoran and Mathers, LLP
A Professional Accounting Firm
245 Water Street, Suite 900
New York, NY 10015

June 30, 1999

Ms. Abby Johnson
Executive Director
The ABC Nonprofit Agency
1500 York Ave., Suite 1000
New York, NY 10028

Dear Ms. Johnson:

Phillips, Corcoran and Mathers, LLP has completed its annual audit of the books of the ABC Nonprofit Agency and have determined that the attached report provides a fair and accurate picture of the agency's financial status for the fiscal year ending December 30, 1998. We came to this conclusion based on employing commonly accepted accounting standards in the industry.

Such standards included a random sampling of both income and expenses that the ABC Nonprofit Agency either received or incurred in the fiscal year in question. While our overall report is believed to be reliable there are some items in the financial statements that we felt merited special attention. These items have been highlighted and addressed point by point in the support documents that follow the financial statements.

We are pleased that you selected our firm to handle your latest audited financial statements.

Sincerely,

Roger Phillips
Partner In Charge

SUPPORT FROM OTHER ORGANIZATIONS

Many corporate funders do not want to provide the so-called pacesetter gift to a nonprofit. Rather, they prefer to step in once the agency has shown that it has the influence and resources to first obtain commitments from other sources, such as the agency's board of directors.

This is almost standard operating procedure for most corporate funders. "Show us that others are committed to your organization and then we can help," is a phrase often heard in the corridors of the corporate philanthropic world. It is easy to see why. Corporations, as a rule, are rather conservative creatures and don't want to go out on a limb. However, if they see a substantial outpouring of support from other companies, individuals, and foundations, they are very likely going to want to jump on the bandwagon.

The ABC Nonprofit Agency
1500 York Avenue, Suite 1000
New York, NY 10028

"The Campaign to Remember"

Contributors List (as of 12/30/99)

Gifts of $10,000 or more
The Robert Smith Charitable Trust
The Gladys and Ethel Hewitt Fund
Mr. Robert Ashworth
Mrs. Margaret Hightower
The NetPlanet.com Corporate Foundation

Gifts of $5,000–$9,999
The Estate of Gertrude Sloan
Leonard Farber and Family
Richard and Abby Johnson
Sid Newell
The Yorktown Development Group

Gifts under $5,000
Nancy Martin Hughes
The Copy Shoppe
Quadry and Associates
Morton and Jean Kaplan
Michael and Peggy Tantleff

LETTERS OF ENDORSEMENT

Sometimes an agency seeking corporate funding will feel compelled to include letters of endorsement as an appendix to their proposal requests. There is nothing inherently wrong with this seemingly good intention but it is a habit akin to including reference letters in a job seeker's application packet. They are nice, and they may not hurt, but they probably do not help all that much for two reasons. First, most endorsement letters may appear to come from a biased source and, second, funders will be much more inclined to give weighting to other more critical components, such as the agency's financial health. Nonetheless, if an agency wishes to include such an item, there is probably no harm done.

Mrs. Robert Evans
259 Park Avenue
New York, NY 10021

August 15, 1999

Ms. Abby Johnson
Executive Director
The ABC Nonprofit Agency
1500 York Avenue, Suite 1000
New York, NY 10028

Dear Abby:

I had the distinct pleasure of meeting you at the agency's downtown Manhattan outpatient clinic this past Monday and learning first-hand some of the very important services that ABC is providing to disadvantaged New Yorkers. I must say that I was impressed with the level of service that your staff was providing to clients during my visit.

Abby, you have been a valuable part of the ABC Agency since its founding twenty-five years ago. It is only through your vision and limitless energy that ABC has reached the point where it is today. I applaud your efforts.

If I can be of assistance to you in any way, such as helping to recruit new volunteers for the thrift shop, please do not hesitate to call.

With fond wishes for another happy and healthy 25 years, I remain

Sincerely yours,

Mrs. Robert Evans

MISSION STATEMENT

Some funders either specifically request or hope that a potential grantee will include the agency's mission statement as a proposal attachment because it gives the funder an overall sense of what the agency is seeking to accomplish.

Most nonprofits already have a mission statement, perhaps one that has been modified several times over the years. Mission statements do not have to be long or involved. Some can be as short as a sentence or two. A mission statement tries to get at the essence of what the non-profit is all about.

The ABC Nonprofit Agency
1500 York Avenue, Suite 1000
New York, NY 10028

Mission Statement

The ABC Nonprofit Agency shall strive to provide the highest level of outpatient service to those New Yorkers most in need of help. We will seek to do this in as compassionate and consistent a manner as possible. We will hold our employees to the highest moral standards in their relationships with our clients.

BIOGRAPHICAL DATA ON KEY STAFF

If the request to a corporate prospect involves funding for a program within an agency, it is always a smart move to include biographical data on key personnel. Such information will be less important if the request is for items such as bricks and mortar projects.

In the hypothetical example created here, the ABC Nonprofit Agency is requesting funds for a building renovation project. In this case it might suffice to include bios on key administrators such as Ms. Johnson.

The ABC Nonprofit Agency
1500 York Avenue, Suite 1000
New York, NY 10028

Profile on Ms. Abby Johnson

Ms. Abby Johnson is currently the Executive Director of the ABC Non-profit Agency, a position she has held since 1985. She is only the second executive director in the agency's history, having succeeded Mr. Ronald Mitchem, who retired in 1984 for health reasons.

Prior to joining the ABC Agency at its founding as the Director of Financial Operations, Ms. Johnson served as Director of Development for the All Saints School in Purchase, New York. Ms. Johnson began her professional working life as a social worker with the City of New York's Department of Health Services in 1967.

Ms. Johnson holds a bachelors degree from Marymount Manhattan College, an MSW from Pace University, and an MBA from New York University. She and her husband, Richard, live in New York with their two children, Mary and Paul.

PRESS RELEASES

Some corporate funders suggest that a prospective grantee include recent press releases either about the agency or its efforts to raise funds. Again, it may be appropriate to include one or two one-page press releases but not to inundate the funder with what appear to be fluff pieces.

The best idea might be to include an in-house press release along with some of the publicity that it generated, such as an article from the local paper.

The ABC Nonprofit Agency
1500 York Avenue, Suite 1000
New York NY 10028

FOR IMMEDIATE RELEASE

For additional information contact
Abby Johnson at (212) 348–2000

New York – October 1 – The ABC Nonprofit Agency announced today the kickoff to the first capital campaign in the agency's history, "The Campaign To Remember," which seeks to raise $500,000 from the local community to help with various projects including the west wing of the agency's downtown Manhattan outpatient clinic. The kickoff follows the culmination of months of planning and a "silent" fund-raising period during which over $100,000 in lead gifts and commitments were obtained.

"We are very excited about the success we have had in the planning stages of this very ambitious campaign," said the agency's current chair of the board, Mr. Robert Ashworth. Added Mr. Ashworth, "The board of directors of the ABC Agency realize that the true creative strength and energy of this nonprofit rests with the untiring efforts of Abby Johnson, ABC's executive director. We firmly support all that Abby has done for ABC and we hope will continue to do in the years ahead."

$250,000 of the total to be raised will be used to renovate and remodel the west wing of the agency's outpatient clinic in lower Manhattan. Lead gifts have been secured from, among others, the NetPlanet.com Corporate Foundation and the Gladys and Ethel Hewitt Fund.

The ABC Agency hopes to complete the Campaign to Remember at the conclusion of the agency's 25th anniversary celebration slated for June of 2001.

###

FORM 990

A corporate funder might also request Form 990, an informational return that all nonprofits with annual gross receipts of $25,000 or more must file with the Internal Revenue Service each year. Similar to the audited financial statements, Form 990 provides yet another snapshot of the organization that a funder may find helpful when reaching a decision on whether or not to approve a grant.

The 1998 ABC Nonprofit Agency's Form 990 appears beginning on the opposite page. An agency's financial office should be able to provide an actual Form 990. Blank forms can be obtained from the IRS by visiting their website at http://www.ustreas.gov.

As of mid-1999, all 501 (c)(3) and (c)(4) organizations are now required to provide copies of their three most recent Form 990s to anyone who requests them. This requirement may be satisfied by posting the forms at the agency's website.

Regarding sample Form 990 for ABC Nonprofit Agency: Please note that the numbers used in this sample 990 are fictitious. Do not attempt to complete your own agency's Form 990 by using this information. Rather, consult a tax advisor.

Form 990

<table>
<tr><td rowspan="3">Form 990

Department of the Treasury
Internal Revenue Service</td><td colspan="2">Return of Organization Exempt From Income Tax
Under section 501(c) of the Internal Revenue Code (except black lung benefit
trust or private foundation) or section 4947(a)(1) nonexempt charitable trust</td><td>OMB No. 1545-0047
1998
This Form is
Open to Public
Inspection</td></tr>
<tr><td colspan="3">Note: The organization may have to use a copy of this return to satisfy state reporting requirements.</td></tr>
</table>

A For the 1998 calendar year, OR tax year period beginning _____, 1998, and ending _____, 19___

| **B** Check if:
☐ Change of address
☐ Initial return
☐ Final return
☐ Amended return
(required also for state reporting) | Please
use IRS
label or
print or
type.
See
Specific
Instruc-
tions. | **C** Name of organization
ABC NONPROFIT AGENCY
Number and street (or P.O. box if mail is not delivered to street address) Room/suite
1500 YORK AVE   1000
City or town, state or country, and ZIP+4
NEW YORK NY 10028-1000 | **D** Employer identification number
12:3456789
E Telephone number
212-540-9234
F Check ▶ ☐ if exemption application is pending |

G Type of organization— ▶☐ Exempt under section 501(c)( ) ◀ (insert number) OR ▶ ☐ section 4947(a)(1) nonexempt charitable trust

Note: *Section 501(c)(3) exempt organizations and 4947(a)(1) nonexempt charitable trusts MUST attach a completed Schedule A (Form 990).*

H(a) Is this a group return filed for affiliates? . . . . ☐ Yes ☐ No

(b) If "Yes," enter the number of affiliates for which this return is filed: . . ▶

(c) Is this a separate return filed by an organization covered by a group ruling? ☐ Yes ☐ No

I If either box in H is checked "Yes," enter four-digit group exemption number (GEN) ▶

J Accounting method: ☒ Cash ☐ Accrual ☐ Other (specify) ▶

K Check here ▶ ☐ if the organization's gross receipts are normally not more than $25,000. The organization need not file a return with the IRS; but if it received a Form 990 Package in the mail, it should file a return without financial data. **Some states require a complete return.**

Note: *Form 990-EZ may be used by organizations with gross receipts less than $100,000 and total assets less than $250,000 at end of year.*

Part I   Revenue, Expenses, and Changes in Net Assets or Fund Balances (See Specific Instructions on page 13.)

1	Contributions, gifts, grants, and similar amounts received:			
a	Direct public support	1a	200,000	
b	Indirect public support	1b		
c	Government contributions (grants)	1c		
d	**Total** (add lines 1a through 1c) (attach schedule of contributors) (cash $ _____ noncash $ _____)		1d	200,000
2	Program service revenue including government fees and contracts (from Part VII, line 93)	2	100,000
3	Membership dues and assessments	3	
4	Interest on savings and temporary cash investments	4	5,000
5	Dividends and interest from securities	5	5,000
6a	Gross rents	6a		
b	Less: rental expenses	6b		
c	Net rental income or (loss) (subtract line 6b from line 6a)	6c	
7	Other investment income (describe ▶)	7	
8a	Gross amount from sale of assets other than inventory . . . . (A) Securities 8a (B) Other		
b	Less: cost or other basis and sales expenses . 8b		
c	Gain or (loss) (attach schedule) 8c		
d	Net gain or (loss) (combine line 8c, columns (A) and (B))	8d	
9	Special events and activities (attach schedule)		
a	Gross revenue (not including $ _____ of contributions reported on line 1a)	9a		
b	Less: direct expenses other than fundraising expenses .	9b		
c	Net income or (loss) from special events (subtract line 9b from line 9a)	9c	
10a	Gross sales of inventory, less returns and allowances . .	10a		
b	Less: cost of goods sold	10b		
c	Gross profit or (loss) from sales of inventory (attach schedule) (subtract line 10b from line 10a) .	10c	
11	Other revenue (from Part VII, line 103)	11	
12	**Total revenue** (add lines 1d, 2, 3, 4, 5, 6c, 7, 8d, 9c, 10c, and 11)	12	310,000
13	Program services (from line 44, column (B))	13	100,000
14	Management and general (from line 44, column (C))	14	95,000
15	Fundraising (from line 44, column (D))	15	45,000
16	Payments to affiliates (attach schedule)	16	
17	**Total expenses** (add lines 16 and 44, column (A))	17	240,000
18	Excess or (deficit) for the year (subtract line 17 from line 12)	18	70,000
19	Net assets or fund balances at beginning of year (from line 73, column (A)) . . .	19	5,000
20	Other changes in net assets or fund balances (attach explanation)	20	
21	Net assets or fund balances at end of year (combine lines 18, 19, and 20)	21	75,000

(left margin labels: Revenue, Expenses, Net Assets)

For Paperwork Reduction Act Notice, see page 1 of the separate instructions.   Cat. No. 11282Y   Form **990** (1998)

Form 990 *(continued)*

Part II	**Statement of Functional Expenses**	All organizations must complete column (A). Columns (B), (C), and (D) are required for section 501(c)(3) and (4) organizations and section 4947(a)(1) nonexempt charitable trusts but optional for others. (See Specific Instructions on page 17.)

Do not include amounts reported on line 6b, 8b, 9b, 10b, or 16 of Part I.		**(A)** Total	**(B)** Program services	**(C)** Management and general	**(D)** Fundraising
22	Grants and allocations (attach schedule) . . (cash $ _____ noncash $ _____)	22				
23	Specific assistance to individuals (attach schedule)	23				
24	Benefits paid to or for members (attach schedule).	24				
25	Compensation of officers, directors, etc. . . .	25				
26	Other salaries and wages	26	165000	70000	55000	40000
27	Pension plan contributions	27	15000	10000	5000	
28	Other employee benefits	28				
29	Payroll taxes	29	10000	5000	3000	2000
30	Professional fundraising fees	30				
31	Accounting fees	31				
32	Legal fees	32				
33	Supplies	33	10000	10000		
34	Telephone	34				
35	Postage and shipping	35				
36	Occupancy	36				
37	Equipment rental and maintenance	37	7000		7000	
38	Printing and publications	38	13000		10000	3000
39	Travel	39	15000	5000	10000	
40	Conferences, conventions, and meetings . .	40	5000		5000	
41	Interest	41				
42	Depreciation, depletion, etc. (attach schedule)	42				
43	Other expenses (itemize): a	43a				
b	....	43b				
c	....	43c				
d	....	43d				
e	....	43e				
44	**Total functional expenses** (add lines 22 through 43) *Organizations completing columns (B)-(D), carry these totals to lines 13-15* .	44	240000	100000	95000	45000

Reporting of Joint Costs.—Did you report in column (B) (Program services) any joint costs from a combined educational campaign and fundraising solicitation? . . . . ▶ ☐ Yes ☒ No
If "Yes," enter **(i)** the aggregate amount of these joint costs $_____ ; **(ii)** the amount allocated to Program services $_____ ;
(iii) the amount allocated to Management and general $_____ ; and **(iv)** the amount allocated to Fundraising $_____

Part III	**Statement of Program Service Accomplishments** (See Specific Instructions on page 20.)

What is the organization's primary exempt purpose? ▶ _TO HELP DISADVANTAGED PEOPLE_

	Program Service Expenses (Required for 501(c)(3) and (4) orgs., and 4947(a)(1) trusts; but optional for others.)
All organizations must describe their exempt purpose achievements in a clear and concise manner. State the number of clients served, publications issued, etc. Discuss achievements that are not measurable. (Section 501(c)(3) and (4) organizations and 4947(a)(1) nonexempt charitable trusts must also enter the amount of grants and allocations to others.)	
a _____	
_____ (Grants and allocations $ _____)	
b _____	
_____ (Grants and allocations $ _____)	
c _____	
_____ (Grants and allocations $ _____)	
d _____	
_____ (Grants and allocations $ _____)	
e Other program services (attach schedule) (Grants and allocations $ _____)	
f **Total of Program Service Expenses** (should equal line 44, column (B), Program services). . . . . ▶	

Form 990 (*continued*)

Part IV   Balance Sheets (See Specific Instructions on page 20.)

			(A) Beginning of year		(B) End of year
Note:	*Where required, attached schedules and amounts within the description column should be for end-of-year amounts only.*				
	45	Cash—non-interest-bearing	*10000*	45	*5000*
	46	Savings and temporary cash investments	*5000*	46	*5000*
	47a	Accounts receivable	47a			
	b	Less: allowance for doubtful accounts . .	47b		47c	
	48a	Pledges receivable	48a			
	b	Less: allowance for doubtful accounts . .	48b		48c	
	49	Grants receivable		49	
	50	Receivables from officers, directors, trustees, and key employees (attach schedule)		50	
Assets	**51a**	Other notes and loans receivable (attach schedule).	51a			
	b	Less: allowance for doubtful accounts . .	51b		51c	
	52	Inventories for sale or use		52	
	53	Prepaid expenses and deferred charges		53	
	54	Investments—securities (attach schedule)	*10000*	54	*5000*
	55a	Investments—land, buildings, and equipment: basis	55a	*100000*		
	b	Less: accumulated depreciation (attach schedule).	55b	*60000*	*40000*	55c	*40000*
	56	Investments—other (attach schedule)		56	
	57a	Land, buildings, and equipment: basis . .	57a			
	b	Less: accumulated depreciation (attach schedule).	57b		57c	
	58	Other assets (describe ▶ _____)		58	
	59	**Total assets** (add lines 45 through 58) (must equal line 74)	*65000*	59	*55000*
Liabilities	60	Accounts payable and accrued expenses	*25000*	60	*15000*
	61	Grants payable		61	
	62	Deferred revenue		62	
	63	Loans from officers, directors, trustees, and key employees (attach schedule).		63	
	64a	Tax-exempt bond liabilities (attach schedule)		64a	
	b	Mortgages and other notes payable (attach schedule)		64b	
	65	Other liabilities (describe ▶ _____)		65	
	66	**Total liabilities** (add lines 60 through 65)	*40000*	66	*40000*
Net Assets or Fund Balances		**Organizations that follow SFAS 117, check here ▶ ☒ and complete lines 67 through 69 and lines 73 and 74.**			
	67	Unrestricted.	*10000*	67	*10000*
	68	Temporarily restricted	*15000*	68	*15000*
	69	Permanently restricted	*25000*	69	*25000*
		Organizations that do not follow SFAS 117, check here ▶ ☐ and complete lines 70 through 74.			
	70	Capital stock, trust principal, or current funds		70	
	71	Paid-in or capital surplus, or land, building, and equipment fund . .		71	
	72	Retained earnings, endowment, accumulated income, or other funds		72	
	73	**Total net assets or fund balances** (add lines 67 through 69 OR lines 70 through 72; column (A) must equal line 19 and column (B) must equal line 21)	*50000*	73	*50000*
	74	**Total liabilities and net assets / fund balances** (add lines 66 and 73)		74	

Form 990 is available for public inspection and, for some people, serves as the primary or sole source of information about a particular organization. How the public perceives an organization in such cases may be determined by the information presented on its return. Therefore, please make sure the return is complete and accurate and fully describes, in Part III, the organization's programs and accomplishments.

Form 990 (*continued*)

Form 990 (1998)   Page **4**

Part IV-A	**Reconciliation of Revenue per Audited Financial Statements with Revenue per Return** (See Specific Instructions, page 22.)	**Part IV-B**	**Reconciliation of Expenses per Audited Financial Statements with Expenses per Return**

Part IV-A

a   Total revenue, gains, and other support per audited financial statements . . ▶   **a**

b   Amounts included on line **a** but not on line 12, Form 990:

  (1) Net unrealized gains on investments . . $_____

  (2) Donated services and use of facilities $_____

  (3) Recoveries of prior year grants . . . $_____

  (4) Other (specify):
  ....
  .... $_____

  Add amounts on lines **(1)** through **(4)** ▶   **b**

c   Line **a** minus line **b**. . . . . ▶   **c**

d   Amounts included on line 12, Form 990 but not on line **a**:

  (1) Investment expenses not included on line 6b, Form 990 . . . $_____

  (2) Other (specify):
  ....
  .... $_____

  Add amounts on lines **(1)** and **(2)** ▶   **d**

e   Total revenue per line 12, Form 990 (line **c** plus line **d**) . . . . . ▶   **e**

Part IV-B

a   Total expenses and losses per audited financial statements . . ▶   **a**

b   Amounts included on line **a** but not on line 17, Form 990:

  (1) Donated services and use of facilities $_____

  (2) Prior year adjustments reported on line 20, Form 990 . . . . $_____

  (3) Losses reported on line 20, Form 990 . $_____

  (4) Other (specify):
  ....
  .... $_____

  Add amounts on lines **(1)** through **(4)** ▶   **b**

c   Line **a** minus line **b** . . . . . ▶   **c**

d   Amounts included on line 17, Form 990 but not on line **a**:

  (1) Investment expenses not included on line 6b, Form 990. . . $_____

  (2) Other (specify):
  ....
  .... $_____

  Add amounts on lines **(1)** and **(2)** ▶   **d**

e   Total expenses per line 17, Form 990 (line **c** plus line **d**) . . . . . ▶   **e**

Part V   List of Officers, Directors, Trustees, and Key Employees (List each one even if not compensated; see Specific Instructions on page 22.)

(A) Name and address	(B) Title and average hours per week devoted to position	(C) Compensation (If not paid, enter -0-.)	(D) Contributions to employee benefit plans & deferred compensation	(E) Expense account and other allowances
ABBY JOHNSON 1500 YORK AVE NY NY 10028	EXECUTIVE DIRECTOR-45	55,000	5,000	5,000
ROBERT ASHWORTH 255 FIFTH AVE NY NY 10019	CHAIRMAN OF THE BOARD - 5	∅		

75   Did any officer, director, trustee, or key employee receive aggregate compensation of more than $100,000 from your organization and all related organizations, of which more than $10,000 was provided by the related organizations? ▶ ☐ Yes ☒ No
If "Yes," attach schedule—see Specific Instructions on page 22.

Form 990 (*continued*)

Part VI   Other Information (See Specific Instructions on page 23.)

		Yes	No
76	Did the organization engage in any activity not previously reported to the IRS? If "Yes," attach a detailed description of each activity . **76**		X
77	Were any changes made in the organizing or governing documents but not reported to the IRS? . . . **77**		X
	If "Yes," attach a conformed copy of the changes.		
78a	Did the organization have unrelated business gross income of $1,000 or more during the year covered by this return? . **78a**		X
b	If "Yes," has it filed a tax return on **Form 990-T** for this year? **78b**		X
79	Was there a liquidation, dissolution, termination, or substantial contraction during the year? If "Yes," attach a statement **79**		
80a	Is the organization related (other than by association with a statewide or nationwide organization) through common membership, governing bodies, trustees, officers, etc., to any other exempt or nonexempt organization? . . . **80a**		X
b	If "Yes," enter the name of the organization ▶		
	.... and check whether it is ☐ exempt **OR** ☐ nonexempt.		

81a Enter the amount of political expenditures, direct or indirect, as described in the instructions for line 81. . . . . |**81a**|

		Yes	No
b	Did the organization file **Form 1120-POL** for this year?. **81b**		X
82a	Did the organization receive donated services or the use of materials, equipment, or facilities at no charge or at substantially less than fair rental value? **82a**		X

b If "Yes," you may indicate the value of these items here. Do not include this amount as revenue in Part I or as an expense in Part II. (See instructions for reporting in Part III.). . . . . |**82b**|

		Yes	No
83a	Did the organization comply with the public inspection requirements for returns and exemption applications? **83a**	X	
b	Did the organization comply with the disclosure requirements relating to quid pro quo contributions? . . **83b**	X	
84a	Did the organization solicit any contributions or gifts that were not tax deductible? **84a**		X
b	If "Yes," did the organization include with every solicitation an express statement that such contributions or gifts were not tax deductible? **84b**		
85	*501(c)(4), (5), or (6) organizations.*—**a** Were substantially all dues nondeductible by members? **85a**		
b	Did the organization make only in-house lobbying expenditures of $2,000 or less? **85b**		
	If "Yes" was answered to either 85a or 85b, **do not** complete 85c through 85h below unless the organization received a waiver for proxy tax owed for the prior year.		

c Dues, assessments, and similar amounts from members . . . . |**85c**|
d Section 162(e) lobbying and political expenditures . . . . |**85d**|
e Aggregate nondeductible amount of section 6033(e)(1)(A) dues notices . . . |**85e**|
f Taxable amount of lobbying and political expenditures (line 85d less 85e) . |**85f**|

		Yes	No
g	Does the organization elect to pay the section 6033(e) tax on the amount in 85f?. **85g**		
h	If section 6033(e)(1)(A) dues notices were sent, does the organization agree to add the amount in 85f to its reasonable estimate of dues allocable to nondeductible lobbying and political expenditures for the following tax year? . . **85h**		

86 *501(c)(7) organizations.*—Enter: **a** Initiation fees and capital contributions included on line 12 . . . . |**86a**|
b Gross receipts, included on line 12, for public use of club facilities. . . . . |**86b**|
87 *501(c)(12) organizations*—Enter:
a Gross income from members or shareholders . . . . |**87a**|
b Gross income from other sources. (Do not net amounts due or paid to other sources against amounts due or received from them.) . . . . |**87b**|

		Yes	No
88	At any time during the year, did the organization own a 50% or greater interest in a taxable corporation or partnership? If "Yes," complete Part IX **88**		

89a *501(c)(3) organizations.*—Enter: Amount of tax imposed on the organization during the year under: section 4911 ▶_____O____ ; section 4912 ▶_____O__ ; section 4955 ▶_____O

		Yes	No
b	*501(c)(3) and 501(c)(4) organizations.*—Did the organization engage in any section 4958 excess benefit transaction during the year? If "Yes," attach a statement explaining each transaction **89b**		X

c Enter: Amount of tax imposed on the organization managers or disqualified persons during the year under sections 4912, 4955, and 4958. . . . . ▶ _____
d Enter: Amount of tax on line 89c, above, reimbursed by the organization. . . . . ▶ _____
90a List the states with which a copy of this return is filed ▶ *NEW YORK* ....
b Number of employees employed in the pay period that includes March 12, 1998 (See instructions.) . . |**90b**|
91 The books are in care of ▶ *HEWITT AND SONS* .... Telephone no. ▶ (*2l2*) *555-1212*
Located at ▶ *1600 FIRST AVENUE* .... ZIP + 4 ▶ *10028-1233*
92 *Section 4947(a)(1) nonexempt charitable trusts filing Form 990 in lieu of* **Form 1041**—Check here . . . . ▶ ☐
and enter the amount of tax-exempt interest received or accrued during the tax year . . ▶ |**92**|

Form 990 (*continued*)

Form 990 (1998)   Page **6**

Part VII — Analysis of Income-Producing Activities (See Specific Instructions on page 27.)

Enter gross amounts unless otherwise indicated.	Unrelated business income		Excluded by section 512, 513, or 514		(E) Related or exempt function income
	(A) Business code	(B) Amount	(C) Exclusion code	(D) Amount	
93 Program service revenue:					
a _____					
b _____					
c _____					
d _____					
e _____					
f Medicare/Medicaid payments					
g Fees and contracts from government agencies					
94 Membership dues and assessments . . .					
95 Interest on savings and temporary cash investments					
96 Dividends and interest from securities . . .					
97 Net rental income or (loss) from real estate:					
a debt-financed property					
b not debt-financed property					
98 Net rental income or (loss) from personal property					
99 Other investment income					
100 Gain or (loss) from sales of assets other than inventory					
101 Net income or (loss) from special events . .					
102 Gross profit or (loss) from sales of inventory .					
103 Other revenue: **a** _____					
b _____					
c _____					
d _____					
e _____					
104 Subtotal (add columns (B), (D), and (E)) . . .					

105 Total (add line 104, columns (B), (D), and (E)) . . . . ▶ _____

Note: *(Line 105 plus line 1d, Part I, should equal the amount on line 12, Part I.)*

Part VIII — Relationship of Activities to the Accomplishment of Exempt Purposes (See Specific Instructions on page 28.)

Line No. ▼	Explain how each activity for which income is reported in column (E) of Part VII contributed importantly to the accomplishment of the organization's exempt purposes (other than by providing funds for such purposes).

Part IX — Information Regarding Taxable Subsidiaries (Complete this Part if the "Yes" box on line 88 is checked.)

Name, address, and employer identification number of corporation or partnership	Percentage of ownership interest	Nature of business activities	Total income	End-of-year assets
	%			
	%			
	%			
	%			

Please Sign Here	Under penalties of perjury, I declare that I have examined this return, including accompanying schedules and statements, and to the best of my knowledge and belief, it is true, correct, and complete. Declaration of preparer (other than officer) is based on all information of whic h preparer has any knowledge. (See General Instruction U, on page 12.)
	▶ *Abby Johnson* 1/28/99 ▶ ABBY JOHNSON, EXECUTIVE DIRECTOR
	Signature of officer Date Type or print name and title.

Paid Preparer's Use Only	Preparer's signature ▶		Date	Check if self-employed ▶ ☐	Preparer's SSN
	Firm's name (or yours if self-employed) and address ▶			EIN ▶	
				ZIP + 4 ▶	

✴

Appendix B

SAMPLE ON-LINE GRANT PROPOSAL FORM*

Printed on the following pages is the Grant Application Form for the Ceridian Corporation, one of a growing number of companies that allows nonprofit organizations to submit a proposal on-line. The form that follows was printed in its entirety directly from the company's website www.ceridian.com. A nonprofit that falls within one of the company's interest areas can complete this form on-line and, when certain that all of the information is correct, hit the "send" button at which time the application would be submitted via the Internet to Ceridian.

---

*Reprinted with permission of Ceridian Corporation. © 1999 Ceridian Corporation.

WHO WE ARE

▶ Printer-friendly version.

CERIDIAN AT A
GLANCE

RECOGNITION
CERIDIAN HAS
RECEIVED

ACQUISITIONS

HISTORY

MISSION AND VALUES

MANAGEMENT

IN THE COMMUNITY

PARTNERSHIPS WITH
SCHOOLS

FREQUENTLY ASKED
NUMBERS

CORPORATE
HEADQUARTERS

Charitable Grant Application

Before you complete this application, please confirm that your request falls within Ceridian's giving focus.

Does your program help people balance their work and home lives?

Is your program associated with health, education or the arts?

If you cannot say yes to either of these questions, please do not apply. If you have answered affirmatively, you may proceed. Remember, most of the gifts Ceridian makes are quite modest so it can provide support to as many organizations as possible.

CONTINUE

▶ Return to top.

 Questions or comments? See **Contact Us**.
Ceridian Home Page

CERIDIAN

WHO WE ARE | CERIDIAN'S BUSINESSES | NEWS ROOM | INVESTOR RELATIONS | CAREERS | CONTACT US | SEARCH | SITE MAP

HOME PAGE

▶ Printer-friendly version.

WHO WE ARE?

CERIDIAN AT A GLANCE

RECOGNITION CERIDIAN HAS RECEIVED

ACQUISITIONS

HISTORY

MISSION AND VALUES

MANAGEMENT

IN THE COMMUNITY

PARTNERSHIPS WITH SCHOOLS

FREQUENTLY ASKED NUMBERS

CORPORATE HEADQUARTERS

Grant Application

Organization Information

Name of Organization

Address 1

Address 2

City

State

Zip

Telephone

Fax

E-mail Address

Individuals Responsible

Name of Top-paid Staff

Title

Direct-dial Phone #

E-mail Address

Contact Person

Title

Direct-dial Phone #

E-mail Address

Organization Description

(2-3 sentences)

```
┌─────────────────────────────────────────┬─▲─┐
│                                          │   │
│                                          │   │
│                                          │   │
│                                          │   │
│                                          │   │
│                                          │─▼─│
└─────────────────────────────────────────┴───┘
```

Board of Directors and Their Affiliations

Name   Affiliation

1. [   ]   [   ]

2. [   ]   [   ]

3. [   ]   [   ]

4. [   ]   [   ]

Private and Foundation Supporters During the Last 12 Months

1. [   ]

2. [   ]

3. [   ]

4. [   ]

        Is your organization an IRS 501(c)(3) not-for-profit?   ○ **Yes**   ◉

        Does your program receive funding from the United Way?   ○ **Yes**   ◉

Amount and Type of Support Requested

       The dollar amount being requested   [$]

       Date by which funds are needed   [   ]

Proposal Summary

Project name (if applying for project support)

[   ]

Summary of the request

```

                                                        ▲



                                                        ▼
```

Project duration

```

```

Population served

```

                                                        ▲



                                                        ▼
```

Budget

Total annual organization budget   `$`

Total project budget (for support other than general   `$`
operation)

Committed and pending funding for requested   `$`
project

Preview Proposal

`  Preview  ` ` Clear `

▶ **Return to top.**

Questions or comments? See **Contact Us**.
© 1999 Ceridian Corporation. All rights reserved.
Ceridian Home Page

CERIDIAN

This is how your grant request will appear.

Read it over carefully and if you need to, use the back button on the bottom of the page go back and make changes.
If you are satisfied, use the send button to send your request.

```
-----------------------------------------------------------------------
CERIDIAN GRANT APPLICATION
-----------------------------------------------------------------------

ORGANIZATION INFORMATION
------------------------


'
Phone:
Fax:
e-mail:

INDIVIDUALS RESPONSIBLE
-----------------------
Name of top paid staff:

Title:
Phone:
E-mail:
Contact person:

Title:
Phone:
E-mail:

ORGANIZATION DESCRIPTION
------------------------


BOARD OF DIRECTORS AND THEIR AFFILIATIONS
-----------------------------------------
/
/
/
/

PRIVATE AND FOUNDATION SUPPORTERS DURING THE LAST 12 MONTHS
----------------------------------------------------------


IRS 501(c)(3) not-for-profit: No
Receives funding from the United Way: No

AMOUNT AND TYPE OF SUPPORT REQUESTED
------------------------------------
Dollar amount being requested: $
Date by which funds are needed:

PROPOSAL SUMMARY
----------------
Project name:
Summary of the request:

Project duration:
Population served:
```

```
BUDGET
------
Total annual organization budget: $
Total project budget (for support other than general operation): $
Committed and pending funding for requested project: $
------------------------------------------------------------------
```

[Send] [Back]

Who We Are | Ceridian's Businesses | News Room | Investor Portfolio | Careers | Contact
Us | Search Our Site | Site Map | Ceridian Home Page

Questions or comments? See Contact Us.

Appendix C

MATCHING GIFT FULFILLMENT VIA PHONE

Companies that allow employees to complete matching gift forms via phone:

Aetna Matching Gift Automated Transaction Center
1-800-327-1851

Ameritech Matching Gift Automated Transaction Center
1-888-744-5638

Anderson Consulting Gift Automated Transaction Center
1-800-723-1465

Arthur Anderson Gift Automated Transaction Center
1-800-723-1465

AT&T Matching Gift Automated Transaction Center
1-800-424-6030

Fannie Mae Matching Gift Automated Transaction Center
1-888-628-2440

General Electric Matching Gift Automated Transaction Center
1-800-462-8244

John Hancock Matching Gift Automated Transaction Center
1-800-628-2454

Lucent Technologies Matching Gift Automated Transaction Center
1-888-999-9033

Appendix D

INTEL MATCHING FORM FOR EDUCATIONAL INSTITUTIONS*

A copy of Intel Corporation's Matching Form for Educational Institutions follows. Many companies match an employee's gift to a nonprofit organization. This form, found at Intel's website, can be accessed only by employees of Intel.

*Reprinted with permission of Intel Corporation.

int̲e̲l̲.
Matching Gifts to Education

Procedure

Step 1: Donor should fill out Section One and send both the form and the contribution to the school.

Step 2: School should complete Section Two and return the form to:

> Intel Foundation, AG1-102
> 5200 N.E. Elam Young Parkway
> Hillsboro, OR 97124-6497

Step 3: The Intel Foundation will verify information on the form and authorize payment to the eligible school. Donor will be notified when the gift has been matched.

Section One: To Be Completed By The Donor (please print or type)

Employee Name:

Last	First	MI

Donor Name (if different from employee)

Last	First	MI

Employee WW ID#	Employee Mail Stop	Donor daytime phone ( )	Donor Status: ☐ Employee ☐ Spouse ☐ Director

School Name

School location (city, state)

Gift was designated to the following specific department or fund (optional)

Amount of Gift	Amount of Gift (write out)	Date of Gift
$	Dollars	

I certify that at the time of this gift I qualify as an eligible employee, spouse, or director of Intel Corporation. I further certify that this gift is my personal contribution and that neither I nor any member of my family nor any individual designated by me has received or will accept a benefit of more than nominal monetary value in return for or as a result of this gift or its matching by the Intel Foundation. I certify that I have not requested matching gift funds from any other source.

Signature of donor _____ Date _____

Section Two: To Be Completed By The School

I certify that this gift was made by the individual named above, and has been received by this institution and that this institution has not provided and will not provide any benefit of more than nominal monetary value to any member of the donor's family, or to any individual designated by the donor in return for or as a result of this gift or its matching by the Intel Foundation.

School Name	Complete Mailing Address

Type of Institution: ☐ Four year college or university ☐ Technical or community college ☐ K-12 (elementary or secondary) ☐ School or university foundation	Tax Status: ☐ Publicly funded institution ☐ Nonprofit independent institution with 501c(3) status ☐ Nonprofit school foundation with 501c(3) status

Printed Name of Authorized Officer	Signature of Authorized Officer

Title of Authorized Officer	Phone and e-mail of authorized officer

Date	Amount Received

Appendix E

MATCHING GIFT INFORMATION FOR THE AMERICAN EXPRESS COMPANY*

The following pages contain the Matching Gift profile for the American Express Company as listed at Higher Education Publication's website *www.hepinc.com*. This particular profile is accessible at no charge to the public at HEP's website.

---

*Reprinted with permission of hep development services. Pages provided by hep at www.hepdevelopment.com.

hep   *GiftPlus Online*

Go back to results list | Main

Foundation #:	470000
Company Name:	American Express Company
Parent Company:	American Express Company
Contact Name:	Ms. Anna Mariella
Position/Title:	Program Associate
Address:	American Express Tower World Financial Center
City, State, Zip:	New York NY 10285-4803
Phone #:	(212) 640-5038

Minimum match: 25.00 **Maximum match:** 5000.00 **Total per employee :** 5000.00 **Gift ratio:** 1:1, 2:1*

Comments: 2:1 for board/volunteer program with $2000 max.

Eligible Personnel/Employee Status

☐ All Employees are eligible
    ☒ All Full-time employees are eligible
    ☐ All Full-time salaried employees are eligible
    ☒ All Part-time salaried employees are eligible
    ☒ Retired employees
    ☐ Spouses of eligible employees
    ☐ Board Of Directors

Employee Affiliation Requirement

☒ Alumni status not required
☐ Must be a graduate of institution
☐ Donor's child or spouse must have attended institution
☐ Membership required
☐ Recipient of patient care

Eligibility:

Educational Institutions

☒ Four-year Colleges and Universities
☒ Graduate and Professional Schools
☒ Community/Junior Colleges
☒ Seminaries
☒ Technical Schools
☒ Secondary Schools
☒ Elementary Schools

Other non-profit 501(c)3 organizations

☒ Charities
☐ Hospitals
☐ Healthcare
☒ Cultural
☐ Social Services
☐ Performing Arts
☐ Public Radio/TV
☐ Religious Organizations
☐ Museums
☐ Environmental/Conservation
☐ Fraternity/Sorority Educational Foundations

Procedure

☐ Donor sends check with form to corporation
☒ Institution/non-profit files form with corporation upon receipt of gift
☐ Donor contacts corporation via telephone
☐ Donor presents evidence of receipt

Distribution

☐ Continuously upon receipt of form(s)
☐ Monthly
☒ Quarterly
☐ Annually
☐ Semi-Annually

Acknowledgement

☐ Gift receipt required with every match
☐ Acknowledgement letter required

Athletics

☐ Will ☒ Will not match gifts to athletic programs
☐ Will ☒ Will not match gifts to athletic scholarship programs
☐ Will ☒ Will not match gifts to athletic building funds

Resource Bibliography

Publishers of Reference Information on Corporate Giving

American Association of Fund-Raising Counsel Trust for Philanthropy
25 West 43rd Street
New York, NY 10036

The Foundation Center
79 Fifth Ave, 8th Floor
New York, NY 10003-3076
www.fdncenter.org
Product Line:
National Directory of Corporate Giving
Corporate Foundation Profiles
FC Search (CD-ROM)

The Taft Group
27500 Drake Rd
Farmington Hills, MI 48331-3535
www.taftgroup.com
Product Line:
Corporate Giving Yellow Pages
Directory of International Corporate Giving in America and Abroad
Corporate Giving Directory
Corporate Giving Watch
Grants on Disc (CD-ROM)
Prospector's Choice (CD-ROM)

The Chronicle of Philanthropy
1255 Twenty-Third Street, NW
Washington, DC 20037
www.philanthropy.com
Product Line:
The Chronicle Guide to Grants
The Non-Profit Handbook

The Oryx Press
4041 N. Central Ave., Suite 700
Phoenix, AZ 85012
www.oryxpress.com
Product Line:
GrantSelect (on-line)
The Grants Database (CD-ROM)

Society for Nonprofit Organizations
6314 Odana Rd Suite 1
Madison, WI 53719
Product Line:
Nonprofit World Funding Alert

Reed Elsevier
P.O. Box 31
Providence, NJ 07974
www.bowker.com
Product Line:
Annual Register of Grant Support

Aspen Publishers
7201 McKinney Circle
Frederick, MD 21704
Product Line:
Corporate Philanthropy Report
GrantScape: Sources on Foundations (CD-ROM)

Council on Foundations
1828 L Street, NW, Suite 300
Washington, DC 20036-5168
www.cof.org
Product Line:
Foundation News and Commentary

The Conference Board
845 Third Avenue
New York, NY 10022–6679
www.conference-board.org

Matching Gift Information

CASE (Council for the Advancement and Support of Education)
1307 New York Ave NW
Suite 1000
Washington, DC 20005–4701
Website: *www.case.org*
Email: matchgifts@case.org
Product Line:
Matching Gift Details, an annual directory that profiles companies with
matching gift programs
Matching Gift Details for Windows, a CD-ROM version of *Details.*
Matching Gift Leaflets, a collection of nonprofit specific direct mail
inserts to include in solicitations to alert prospects that they can have
their gift matched by their employers.

Higher Education Publications, Inc. (HEP)
6400 Arlington Blvd, Suite 648
Falls Church, VA 22042
Website: *www.hepinc.com*
Email: *info@hepinc.com*
Product Line:
GiftPlus Corporate Matching Gift Database
Matching Gift Register

Blackbaud
4401 Belle Oaks Dr.
Charleston, SC 29405–8530
Website: *www.blackbaud.com*
Email: *sales@blackbaud.com*
Product Line:
Matchfinder

Software for Grantmakers

Microedge
619 West 54th Street, 10th Floor
New York, NY 10019-3545
Product Line:
Gifts for Windows
Website: *www.microedge.com*
Email: *info@microedge.com*

Companies Specializing in Cause-Related Marketing

The Brighton Group
Star Route
Brighton, UT 84121

IEG, Inc. (Events International Group)
640 North LaSalle St, Suite 600
Chicago, IL 60610–3777
Publishers of the *IEG Sponsorship Report*, a bi-weekly
newsletter on sports, arts, events, and cause marketing.
Website: *www.sponsorship.com*
E-mail: *ieg@sponsorship.com*

Cone Communications
90 Canal Street
Boston, MA 02114
Website: *www.conenet.com*
E-mail: *Carol_Cone@conenet.com*

In-Kind Companies

Gifts-In-Kind International
333 North Fairfax Street
Alexandria, VA 22314
Website: *www.GiftsInKind.org*
E-mail: *ProductDonations@GiftsInKind.org*

National Association for the Exchange of Industrial Resources
P.O. Box 8076
540 Frontage Rd
Northfield, IL 60093

Articles of Interest

Foster, Vincent S., **Donors for Doers**, *Fund Raising Management Magazine*, June, 1989.

Katz, Lee, **Corporate Support and Winning Proposals**, *Fund Raising Management Magazine*, June, 1990.

Index

Visit us on the World Wide Web

NONPROFIT
Resource Center

www.wiley.com/nonprofit

Our nonprofit website features:

• **A nonprofit catalogue** where you can order and search for titles online. View book and author information about our management, law/tax, fund-raising, accounting and finance titles.

• **A threaded discussion forum**, which will provide you and your colleagues with the chance to ask questions, share knowledge, and debate issues important to your organization and the sector.

• **Over 500 free forms and worksheets** to help run any nonprofit organization more efficiently and effectively. Forms are updated monthly to cover a new key area of nonprofit management.

• **Useful links** to many nonprofit resources online.

The Wiley Nonprofit Series brings together an extraordinary team of experts in the fields of nonprofit management, fund raising, law, accounting, and finance. This website highlights our new books, which present the best, most innovative practices being used in the nonprofit sector today. It also highlights our established works, which through their use in the day-to-day operations of thousands of nonprofits, have proven themselves to be invaluable to any nonprofit looking to raise more money or improve their operations, while still remaining in compliance with all rules and regulations.

For nearly 200 years, Wiley has prided itself on being a publisher of books known for thoroughness, rigor, and readability. Please browse the website. You are sure to find valued titles that you need to navigate the new world of nonprofit action.

Wiley Nonprofit Series